Contents

Introduction

When we finished *Best in Show: Knit Your Own Dog*, we thought that we had covered a pretty comprehensive assortment, but there are many more popular breeds of dog than we ever imagined. People have expressed outrage at the omission of their particular pet and we can only apologise and hope to remedy this with *Best in Show: 25 More Dogs to Knit*.

Here, we offer you yet more dogs, another 25 to knit. There were various glaring omissions in our first book: very popular dogs like the Retriever, Boxer and Border Terrier, which we have now created for you. We know that we still haven't covered all breeds, but we hope with the 50 canines now available we have included most basic dog types. If you have a very specialist dog which we haven't included, and there will be some (over the past two years we have been asked for Lancashire Heelers, Coton de Tulears, Ovcharkas and Glen of Imaal Terriers), we hope that with your own

knitting skills you will be able to adapt one of our patterns to make your own unique dog.

There are many uses for the small knitted dog: people have told us that they can be used to provide consolation for a friend who has lost their dog, comfort a homesick child with a tiny knitted version of a much loved pet, fob off the family who are braying for a pet, re-create their long-dead childhood friend, or mount their own miniature Crufts.

You can knit the dogs in any yarn – if you use larger needles and thicker wool you will get a larger dog – make them in your own particular dog's colours, make the legs longer or shorter, change the shape of the ears, trim a loopy coat, make the tail docked or not; please do play with the patterns. It's your dog, so give it its unique characteristics and create your very own pêt a pòrter...

Joanna and Sally

Toy

Chihuahua

Officially the world's smallest breed, the Chihuahua's history is shrouded in mystery. Possibly bred by Aztecs, it is named after the Mexican state. However, it could have been bred in Europe, as one of the earliest depictions of a remarkably Chihuahua-like dog appears in a 15th-century fresco in the Sistine Chapel, *Trials of Moses*, by Sandro Botticelli. Apart from the obvious Paris Hilton and Britney Spears, Mickey Rourke had an adored Chihuahua called Loki, whom he described as 'the love of my life'.

Chihuahua

Neat and compact, this is one of the simpler dogs to knit.

Measurements

Length: 13cm (5in)
Height to top of head: 10cm (4in)

Materials

- Pair of 2¾mm (US 2) knitting needles
- Double-pointed 2¾mm (US 2) knitting needles (for holding stitches and for tail)
- 15g (½oz) of Rowan Cashsoft 4ply in Arran 456 (ar)
- 5g (⅙oz) of Rowan Cashsoft 4ply in Cream 433 (cr)
- Small amount of Rowan Cashsoft 4ply in Redwood 429 (re) for collar
- 3 pipecleaners for legs and tail
- Tiny amount of Rowan Pure Wool 4ply in Black 404 (bl) for eyes and nose
- 2 tiny black beads for eyes and sewing needle and black thread for sewing on

Abbreviations

See page 172.
See page 172 for Colour Knitting.
See page 172 for I-cord Technique.
See page 172 for Wrap and Turn Method.

Head

The nose is smaller than that of most of the dogs, and the Chihuahua has bead and French knot eyes.

Right Back Leg

With ar, cast on 7 sts.
Beg with a k row, work 3 rows st st.
Row 4: Inc, p2tog, p1, p2tog, inc. *(7 sts)*
Work 5 rows st st.
Row 10: P2tog, [inc] 3 times, p2tog. *(8 sts)*
Row 11: Inc, k6, inc. *(10 sts)*
Work 4 rows st st.
Row 16: Inc, p8, inc. *(12 sts)*
Row 17: Inc, k10, inc. *(14 sts)*
Row 18: Inc, p12, inc. *(16 sts)*
Row 19: Knit.
Row 20: Purl.*
Row 21: Cast (bind) off 8 sts, k to end (hold 8 sts on spare needle for Right Side of Body).

Left Back Leg

Work as for Right Back Leg to *.
Row 21: K8, cast (bind) off 8 sts (hold 8 sts on spare needle for Left Side of Body).

Right Front Leg

With ar, cast on 7 sts.
Beg with a k row, work 3 rows st st.
Row 4: P2tog, inc, p1, inc, p2tog. *(7 sts)*
Work 10 rows st st.
Row 15: Inc, k2, inc, k2, inc. *(10 sts)*
Row 16: Purl.**
Row 17: Cast (bind) off 5 sts, k to end (hold
5 sts on spare needle for Right Side of Body).

Left Front Leg

Work as for Right Front Leg to **.
Row 17: K5, cast (bind) off 5 sts (hold 5 sts
on spare needle for Left Side of Body).

Right Side of Body

Row 1: With ar, cast on 1 st, with RS facing
k5 from spare needle of Right Front Leg,
cast on 4 sts. *(10 sts)*
Row 2: Purl.
Row 3: Inc, k9, cast on 3 sts. *(14 sts)*
Row 4: Purl.
Row 5: Inc, k13, cast on 3 sts, with RS
facing k8 from spare needle of Right Back
Leg. *(26 sts)*
Work 3 rows st st.
Row 9: Inc, k25. *(27 sts)*
Work 3 rows st st.
Row 13: Inc, k26. *(28 sts)*
Row 14: Purl.
Row 15: K26, k2tog. *(27 sts)*
Row 16: P3 (hold 3 sts on spare needle for
tail), p24.
Row 17: K8 (hold 8 sts on spare needle for
right neck), cast (bind) off 16 sts.

Left Side of Body

Row 1: With ar, cast on 1 st, with WS facing
p5 from spare needle of Left Front Leg, cast
on 4 sts. *(10 sts)*
Row 2: Knit.
Row 3: Inc, p9, cast on 3 sts. *(14 sts)*
Row 4: Knit.
Row 5: Inc, p13, cast on 3 sts, with WS
facing p8 from spare needle of Left Back Leg.
(26 sts)
Work 3 rows st st.
Row 9: Inc, p25. *(27 sts)*
Work 3 rows st st.
Row 13: Inc, p26. *(28 sts)*
Row 14: Knit.
Row 15: P26, p2tog. *(27 sts)*
Row 16: K3 (hold 3 sts on spare needle for
tail), k24.
Row 17: P8 (hold 8 sts on spare needle for
left neck), cast (bind) off 16 sts.

Body
As this is a delicate dog,
don't overstuff the body.

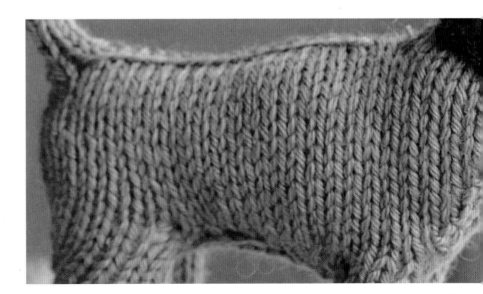

Legs

Sew the leg seams very neatly to make the Chihuahua's shapely legs look good.

Neck and Head

Row 1: With ar and with RS facing, k8 held for neck from spare needle of Right Side of Body, then k8 held for neck from spare needle of Left Side of Body. *(16 sts)*
Row 2: P7, p2tog, p7. *(15 sts)*
Row 3: Knit.
Row 4: P1, inc, p11, inc, p1. *(17 sts)*
Row 5: K14, wrap and turn (leave 3 sts on left-hand needle unworked).
Row 6: Working top of head on centre 11 sts only, p11, w&t.
Row 7: K11, w&t.
Row 8: P11, w&t.
Row 9: K11, w&t.
Row 10: P11, w&t.
Row 11: Knit across all sts. *(17 sts in total)*
Row 12: Purl.
Join in cr.
Row 13: K7ar, k3cr, k4ar, w&t (leave 3 sts on left-hand needle unworked).
Row 14: Working top of head on centre 11 sts only, p4ar, p3cr, p4ar, w&t.
Row 15: K4ar, k3cr, k4ar, w&t.
Row 16: P4ar, p3cr, p4ar, w&t.
Row 17: K4ar, k3cr, k7ar. *(17 sts in total)*
Row 18: [P2togar] 3 times, p5cr, [p2togar] 3 times. *(11 sts)*
Row 19: K1ar, [k2togcr] twice, k1cr, [k2togcr] twice, k1ar. *(7 sts)*
Cont in cr.
Row 20: Purl.
Row 21: K2tog, sk2po, k2tog. *(3 sts)*
Row 22: P3tog and fasten off.

Tail

Row 1: With two double-pointed needles and ar and with RS facing, k3 held for tail from spare needle of Left Side of Body, then k3 held for tail from spare needle of Right Side of Body. *(6 sts)*
Work in i-cord as folls:
Knit 8 rows.
Row 10: K2tog, k2, k2tog. *(4 sts)*
Knit 7 rows.
Row 18: [K2tog] twice. *(2 sts)*
Row 19: K2tog and fasten off.

Tummy

With ar, cast on 1 st.
Row 1: Inc. *(2 sts)*
Row 2: Purl.
Row 3: [Inc] twice. *(4 sts)*
Row 4: Purl.
Row 5: Inc, k2, inc. *(6 sts)*
Row 6: Purl.
Work 42 rows st st.
Join in cr.
Row 49: K2ar, k2cr, k2ar.
Row 50: P1ar, p4cr, p1ar.
Cont in cr.
Work 4 rows st st.
Row 55: K2tog, k2, k2tog. *(4 sts)*
Work 7 rows st st.
Row 63: [K2tog] twice. *(2 sts)*
Row 64: P2tog and fasten off.

Ear

(make 2 the same)
With ar, cast on 6 sts.
Beg with a k row, work 6 rows st st.
Row 7: K2tog, k2, k2tog. *(4 sts)*
Row 8: Purl.
Row 9: [K2tog] twice. *(2 sts)*
Row 10: P2tog and fasten off.

Collar

With re, cast on 20 sts.
Knit one row.
Cast (bind) off.

To Make Up

See also diagram and notes on page 173.

SEWING IN ENDS Sew in ends, leaving ends from cast on and cast (bound) off rows for sewing up.

LEGS With WS together, fold leg in half. Starting at paw, sew up leg on RS.

BODY Sew along back of dog to tail.

TAIL Cut a pipecleaner 2.5cm (1in) longer than tail. Roll a little stuffing around pipecleaner and slip into tail. Protruding bare end of pipecleaner will vanish into body stuffing.

TUMMY Sew cast on row of tummy to top of dog's bottom (just below tail), and sew cast (bound) off row to chin. Ease and sew tummy to fit body. Leave a 2.5cm (1in) gap between front and back legs on one side.

STUFFING Pipecleaners are used to stiffen the legs and help bend them into shape. Fold a pipecleaner into a 'U' shape and measure against front two legs. Cut to approximately fit, leaving an extra 2.5cm (1in) at both ends. Fold these ends over to stop pipecleaner poking out of paws. Roll a little stuffing around pipecleaner and slip into body, one end down each front leg. Repeat with second pipecleaner and back legs. Starting at the head, stuff the dog firmly, then sew up the gap. Mould body into shape.

EARS Sew cast on row of each ear to side of dog's head, with 5 sts between ears and with wrong side of ears facing forwards.

EYES With bl, sew 2-loop French knots positioned as in photograph. Sew beads on top of French knots.

NOSE With bl, embroider nose in satin stitch.

COLLAR Sew ends of collar together and pop over head.

Bichon Frise

Fluffy, fun-loving and affectionate, the Bichon Frise belongs to a family of breeds that includes the Havanese, Maltese and Bolognese. Originally from the Mediterranean, the Bichon was used as barter by sailors, thereby spreading the breed throughout the world. Bichon Frise means 'curly lapdog' in old French, and this exotic little dog appears in several of Goya's paintings. Having had a position at court for several centuries, by the 19th century it had fallen out of fashion and was reduced to performing in circuses. Now hugely back in favour, Barbra Streisand and Coleen Rooney are enthusiasts.

Bichon Frise

The Bichon is sewn up with the purl side on the outside to give a curly feel to the coat.

Measurements

Length: 14cm (5½in)
Height to top of head: 13cm (5in)

Materials

- Pair of 2¾mm (US 2) knitting needles
- Double-pointed 2¾mm (US 2) knitting needles (for holding stitches)
- 15g (½oz) of Rowan Pure Wool 4ply in Snow 412 (sn)
- 10g (¼oz) of Rowan Kidsilk Haze in Cream 634 (cr)
- NOTE: use one strand of sn and cr held together, and this is called snc
- Small amount of Rowan Cashsoft 4ply in Toxic 459 (tx) for collar
- 3 pipecleaners for legs and tail
- Tiny amount of Rowan Pure Wool 4ply in Black 404 (bl) for eyes and nose

Abbreviations

See page 172.
See page 172 for Wrap and Turn Method.
See page 172 for Loopy Stitch. Work 2-finger loopy stitch throughout this pattern, and take the loops through to the purl side of the knitting.

Right Back Leg

With snc, cast on 7 sts.
Beg with a k row, work 2 rows st st.
Row 3: Inc, k2tog, k1, k2tog, inc. *(7 sts)*
Row 4: Purl.
Row 5: K2tog, k3, k2tog. *(5 sts)*
Row 6: Purl.
Row 7: Inc, k3, inc. *(7 sts)*
Work 3 rows st st.*
Row 11: K2, inc, p1, inc, k2. *(9 sts)*
Row 12: P3, inc, p1, inc, p3. *(11 sts)*
Row 13: K4, inc, k1, inc, k4. *(13 sts)*
Row 14: Purl.
Row 15: Inc, k11, inc. *(15 sts)*
Row 16: Purl.**
Row 17: K8, cast (bind) off 7 sts (hold 8 sts on spare needle for Right Side of Body).

Left Back Leg

Work as for Right Back Leg to **.
Row 17: Cast (bind) off 7 sts, k to end (hold 8 sts on spare needle for Left Side of Body).

Right Front Leg

Work as for Right Back Leg to *.
Row 11: Inc, k5, inc. *(9 sts)*
Row 12: Purl.
Row 13: K3, inc, k1, inc, k3. *(11 sts)*
Row 14: Purl.***
Row 15: K6, cast (bind) off 5 sts (hold 6 sts on spare needle for Right Side of Body).

Left Front Leg

Work as for Right Front Leg to ***.
Row 15: Cast (bind) off 5 sts, k to end (hold 6 sts on spare needle for Left Side of Body).

Right Side of Body

Row 1: With snc, cast on 1 st, with RS (purl side) facing p6 from spare needle of Right Front Leg, cast on 8 sts. *(15 sts)*
Row 2: Knit.

Row 3: Inc, p14, cast on 5 sts, with RS (purl side) facing p8 from spare needle of Right Back Leg, cast on 1 st. *(30 sts)*
Row 4: Knit.
Row 5: Inc, p29. *(31 sts)*
Work 7 rows st st.
Row 13: Inc, p30. *(32 sts)*
Row 14: Knit.
Row 15: P30, p2tog. *(31 sts)*
Row 16: K4 (hold 4 sts on spare needle for tail), cast (bind) off 18 sts, k to end (hold 9 sts on spare needle for right neck).

Left Side of Body

Row 1: With snc, cast on 1 st, with WS (knit side) facing k6 from spare needle of Left Front Leg, cast on 8 sts. *(15 sts)*
Row 2: Purl.
Row 3: Inc, k14, cast on 5 sts, with WS (knit side) facing k8 from spare needle of Left Back Leg, cast on 1 st. *(30 sts)*
Row 4: Purl.
Row 5: Inc, k29. *(31 sts)*
Work 7 rows st st.
Row 13: Inc, k30. *(32 sts)*
Row 14: Purl.
Row 15: K30, k2tog. *(31 sts)*
Row 16: P4 (hold 4 sts on spare needle for tail), cast (bind) off 18 sts, p to end (hold 9 sts on spare needle for left neck).

Neck and Head

Row 1: With snc and with RS (purl side) facing, p9 held for neck from spare needle of Right Side of Body, then p9 held for neck from spare needle of Left Side of Body. *(18 sts)*

Row 2: K4, k2tog, k6, k2tog, k4. *(16 sts)*

Row 3: Purl.

Row 4: K4, k2tog, k4, k2tog, k4. *(14 sts)*

Row 5: Purl.

Row 6: K11, wrap and turn (leave 3 sts on left-hand needle unworked).

Row 7: Working top of head on centre 8 sts only, p8, w&t.

Row 8: K8, w&t.

Row 9: P8, w&t.

Row 10: K3, loopy st 2, k3, w&t.

Row 11: P8, w&t.

Row 12: K2, loopy st 4, k5. *(14 sts in total)*

Row 13: Purl.

Row 14: K4, loopy st 6, k1, w&t (leave 3 sts on left-hand needle unworked).

Row 15: P8, w&t.

Row 16: K1, loopy st 6, k1, w&t.

Row 17: P8, w&t.

Row 18: K1, loopy st 6, k1, w&t.

Row 19: P8, w&t.

Row 20: K2, loopy st 4, k5. *(14 sts in total)*

Row 21: P2, p2tog, p2, p2tog, p2, p2tog, p2. *(11 sts)*

Row 22: K2, k2tog, k3, k2tog, k2. *(9 sts)*

Work 3 rows st st.

Row 26: K1, loopy st 2, k3, loopy st 2, k1.

Row 27: Purl.

Row 28: K2tog, loopy st 2, k1, loopy st 2, k2tog. *(7 sts)*

Cast (bind) off.

Head

Once knitted, the loops need to be moved over to the purl side of the knitting.

Tail

Row 1: With snc and with RS (purl side) facing, p4 held for tail from spare needle of Left Side of Body, then p4 held for tail from spare needle of Right Side of Body. *(8 sts)*
Row 2: Knit.
Row 3: Purl.
Row 4: K2tog, k1, [inc] twice, k1, k2tog. *(8 sts)*
Work 3 rows st st.
Row 8: K1, loopy st 6, k1.
Row 9: Purl.
Rep rows 8–9 once more.
Row 12: K2tog, loopy st 4, k2tog. *(6 sts)*
Row 13: Purl.
Row 14: K1, loopy st 4, k1.
Row 15: Purl.
Row 16: K2tog, loopy st 2, k2tog. *(4 sts)*
Row 17: Purl.
Row 18: [K2tog] twice. *(2 sts)*
Row 19: P2tog and fasten off.

Tummy

With snc, cast on 4 sts.
Beg with a k row, work 20 rows st st.
Row 21: K1, [inc] twice, k1. *(6 sts)*
Work 15 rows st st.
Row 37: K2tog, k2, k2tog. *(4 sts)*
Work 3 rows st st.
Row 41: Inc, k2, inc. *(6 sts)*
Work 17 rows st st.
Row 59: K2tog, k2, k2tog. *(4 sts)*
Work 11 rows st st.
Row 71: [K2tog] twice. *(2 sts)*
Row 72: P2tog and fasten off.

Ear

(make 2 the same)
With snc, cast on 4 sts.
Beg with a k row, work 2 rows st st.
Row 3: Loopy st 4.
Row 4: Purl.
Rep rows 3–4 once more.
Row 7: Loopy st 4.
Cast (bind) off.

Collar

With tx, cast on 24 sts.
Knit one row.
Cast (bind) off.

Body

The combination of Pure Wool and Kidsilk Haze yarns works well for dogs with fluffy coats.

To Make Up

See also diagram and notes on page 173. Sew up with purl side as outside of dog.

SEWING IN ENDS Sew in ends, leaving ends from cast on and cast (bound) off rows for sewing up.

LEGS With WS together, fold leg in half. Starting at paw, sew up leg on RS.

BODY Sew along back of dog to tail. Sew from tip of tail down to bottom of dog's bottom.

TAIL Cut a pipecleaner 2.5cm (1in) longer than tail. Roll a little stuffing around pipecleaner, wrap tail around pipecleaner and sew up tail on RS. Protruding end of pipecleaner will vanish into body stuffing.

HEAD Fold cast (bound) off row of head in half and sew from nose to chin.

TUMMY Sew cast on row of tummy to bottom of dog's bottom (where back legs begin), and sew cast (bound) off row to chin. Ease and sew tummy to fit body. Leave a 2.5cm (1in) gap between front and back legs on one side.

STUFFING Pipecleaners are used to stiffen the legs and help bend them into shape. Fold a pipecleaner into a 'U' shape and measure against front two legs. Cut to approximately fit, leaving an extra 2.5cm (1in) at both ends. Fold these ends over to stop pipecleaner poking out of paws. Roll a little stuffing around pipecleaner and slip into body, one end down each front leg. Repeat with second pipecleaner and back legs. Starting at the head, stuff the dog firmly, then sew up the gap. Mould body into shape.

EARS Sew cast on row of each ear to sides of dog's head, just below the edge of loopy stitch topknot.

EYES With bl, sew 3-loop French knots positioned as in photograph.

NOSE With bl, embroider nose in satin stitch.

COLLAR Sew ends of collar together and pop over head.

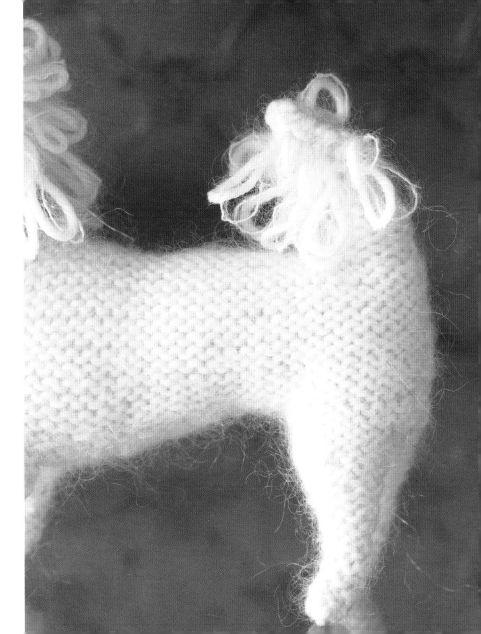

Shih Tzu

Also known as the Lion Dog – originally from Tibet, but very popular in China – Shih Tzus were brought to Britain in the 1930s by Sir Douglas and Lady Brownrigg and Miss Hutchins. The Shih Tzu is assertive and engaging, often described as spunky, but they can be snappish if peeved. They don't need much exercise, but do need an enormous amount of grooming. As well Anna Nicole Smith, Geri Halliwell and Beyoncé, David Hasselhoff, Bill Gates and the Dalai Lama are also Shih Tzu owners.

Shih Tzu

Do perfect the loopy stitch technique before attempting to knit this pert dog.

Measurements

Length: 17cm (6¾in)
Height to top of head: 15cm (6in)

Materials

- Pair of 2¾mm (US 2) knitting needles
- Double-pointed 2¾mm (US 2) knitting needles (for holding stitches)
- 15g (½oz) of Rowan Baby Alpaca DK in Jacob 205 (ja)
- 25g (1oz) of Rowan Baby Alpaca DK in Lincoln 209 (li)
- 3 pipecleaners for legs and tail
- Tiny amount of Rowan Pure Wool 4ply in Black 404 (bl) for eyes and nose
- Tiny amount of Rowan Cashsoft 4ply in Pretty 460 (pr) for bow

Abbreviations

See page 172.
See page 172 for Colour Knitting.
See page 172 for Wrap and Turn Method.
See page 172 for Loopy Stitch. Work 2-finger loopy stitch on the legs and 4-finger loopy stitch on all other parts.
NOTE: this dog has no ears.

Right Back Leg

With ja, cast on 11 sts.
Beg with a k row, work 2 rows st st.
Row 3: K3, k2tog, k1, k2tog, k3. *(9 sts)*
Work 5 rows st st.
Break ja and cont in li.
Row 9: K1, loopy st 7, k1.
Row 10: Purl.*
Row 11: Inc, k7, inc. *(11 sts)*
Row 12: Purl.
Row 13: Inc, k9, inc. *(13 sts)*
Row 14: Purl.**
Row 15: Cast (bind) off 7 sts, k to end (hold 6 sts on spare needle for Right Side of Body).

Left Back Leg

Work as for Right Back Leg to **.
Row 15: K6, cast (bind) off 7 sts (hold 6 sts on spare needle for Left Side of Body).

Right Front Leg

Work as for Right Back Leg to *, but working in ja throughout.
Row 11: Cast (bind) off 4 sts, k to end (hold 5 sts on spare needle for Right Side of Body).

Left Front Leg

Work as for Right Back Leg to *, but working in ja throughout.
Row 11: K5, cast (bind) off 4 sts (hold 5 sts on spare needle for Left Side of Body).

Right Side of Body

Row 1: With ja, cast on 1 st, with RS facing k5 from spare needle of Right Front Leg, cast on 6 sts. *(12 sts)*
Row 2: Purl.
Row 3: K12, cast on 6 sts. *(18 sts)*
Row 4: Purl.
Join in li.
Row 5: K10ja, k8li, cast on 6 sts li. *(24 sts)*
Row 6: P14li, p10ja.

Row 7: K1ja, loopy st 9ja, loopy st 14li, cast on 5 sts li, k6li from spare needle of Right Back Leg. *(35 sts)*
Row 8: P25li, p10ja.
Row 9: K10ja, k25li.
Row 10: P25li, p10ja.
Row 11: K1ja, loopy st 9ja, loopy st 24li, k1li.
Row 12: P25li, p10ja.
Row 13: K10ja, k23li, k2togli. *(34 sts)*
Row 14: P24li, p10ja.
Row 15: K10ja, k22li, k2togli. *(33 sts)*
Row 16: P23li, p10ja.
Row 17: K1ja, loopy st 9ja, loopy st 22li, k1li.
Row 18: Cast (bind) off 23 sts li and 1 st ja, p9ja icos (hold 9 sts on spare needle for right neck).

Left Side of Body

Row 1: With ja, cast on 1 st, with WS facing p5 from spare needle of Left Front Leg, cast on 6 sts. *(12 sts)*
Row 2: Knit.
Row 3: P12, cast on 6 sts. *(18 sts)*
Row 4: Knit.
Join in li.
Row 5: P10ja, p8li, cast on 6 sts li. *(24 sts)*
Row 6: K14li, k10ja.
Row 7: P10ja, p14li, cast on 5 sts li, with WS facing p6li from spare needle of Left Back Leg. *(35 sts)*
Row 8: K1li, loopy st 24li, loopy st 9ja, k1ja.
Row 9: P10ja, p25li.
Row 10: K25li, k10ja.
Row 11: P10ja, p25li.
Row 12: K1li, loopy st 24li, loopy st 9ja, k1ja.
Row 13: P10ja, p23li, p2togli. *(34 sts)*
Row 14: K24li, k10ja.
Row 15: P10ja, p22li, p2togli. *(33 sts)*
Row 16: K23li, k10ja.
Row 17: P10ja, p23li.
Row 18: Loopy st and at the same time cast (bind) off 23 sts li and 1 st ja, k9ja icos (hold 9 sts on spare needle for left neck).

Body
Make sure the loops are long to give the coat a silky, luxurious feel.

Neck and Head

Row 1: With ja and with RS facing, k9 held for neck from spare needle of Right Side of Body and loopy st 9 held for neck from spare needle of Left Side of Body. *(18 sts)*

Row 2: Purl.

Join in li.

Row 3: K1ja, loopy st 4ja, loopy st 8li, loopy st 4ja, k1ja.

Row 4: P4ja, p10li, p4ja.

Row 5: K4ja, loopy st 10li, wrap and turn (leave 4 sts on left-hand needle unworked).

Row 6: Working top of head on centre 10 sts only, p10li, w&t.

Row 7: Loopy st 10ja, w&t.

Row 8: P10li, w&t.

Row 9: Loopy st 10li, k4ja. *(18 sts in total)*

Row 10: P4ja, p10li, p4ja.

Row 11: K1ja, loopy st 3ja, loopy st 10li, loopy st 3ja, k1ja.

Row 12: P2ja, p14li, p2ja.

Row 13: K2ja, loopy st 12li, w&t (leave 4 sts on left-hand needle unworked).

Row 14: Working top of head on centre 10 sts only, p10li, w&t.

Row 15: Loopy st 10li, w&t.

Row 16: P10li, w&t.

Row 17: Loopy st 12li, k2ja. *(18 sts in total)*

Row 18: [P2togja] 3 times, [p2togli] 3 times, [p2togja] 3 times. *(9 sts)*

Cont in ja.

Row 19: Knit.

Row 20: P1, p2tog, p3, p2tog, p1. *(7 sts)*

Row 21: Loopy st 3, k1, loopy st 3.

Row 22: P1, p2tog, p1, p2tog, p1. *(5 sts)*

Cast (bind) off.

Tail

With ja, cast on 8 sts.

Beg with a k row, work 2 rows st st.

Join in li.

Row 3: K1ja, loopy st 2ja, loopy st 4li, k1li.

Row 4: P5li, p3ja.

Row 5: K3ja, k5li.

Row 6: P5li, p3ja.

Rep rows 3–6, 4 times more.

Row 23: K2togja, loopy st 1ja, loopy st 3li, k2togli. *(6 sts)*

Cast (bind) off.

Tummy

With ja, cast on 5 sts.

Beg with a k row, work 46 rows st st.

Row 47: K2tog, k1, k2tog. *(3 sts)*

Row 48: P3tog and fasten off.

Head

Use pink yarn to scoop up and tie the dog's topknot.

To Make Up

See also diagram and notes on page 173.

SEWING IN ENDS Sew in ends, leaving ends from cast on and cast (bound) off rows for sewing up.

LEGS With WS together, fold leg in half. Starting at paw, sew up leg on RS.

BODY Sew along back of dog and around bottom.

HEAD Fold cast (bound) off row of head in half and sew 1cm (⅜in) down nose. Fold final row of nose back on itself and sew down with 2 horizontal satin sts to approx row 21 of head.

TUMMY Sew cast on row of tummy to bottom of dog's bottom (where back legs begin), and sew cast (bound) off row to chin. Ease and sew tummy to fit body. Leave a 2.5cm (1in) gap between front and back legs on one side.

STUFFING Pipecleaners are used to stiffen the legs and help bend them into shape. Fold a pipecleaner into a 'U' shape and measure against front two legs. Cut to approximately fit, leaving an extra 2.5cm (1in) at both ends. Fold these ends over to stop pipecleaner poking out of paws. Roll a little stuffing around pipecleaner and slip into body, one end down each front leg. Repeat with second pipecleaner and back legs. Starting at the head, stuff the dog firmly, then sew up the gap. Mould body into shape.

TAIL Cut a pipecleaner 2.5cm (1in) longer than tail. Roll a little stuffing around pipecleaner, wrap tail around pipecleaner and sew up on RS. Push protruding pipecleaner end into dog where back meets bottom and sew tail on. Bend into characteristic curl.

EYES With bl, sew 3-loop French knots just above nose.

LOOPS Cut all loops and trim as desired.

TOPKNOT Scoop up about 8 tufts from top of head and secure with 2 lengths of pr tied in a bow.

Wire-haired Dachshund

Extrovert, bold and clever, Wire-haired Dachshunds are also self-opinionated and can be rather vocal. H.L. Mencken described the Dachshund as 'a half-a-dog high and a dog-and-a-half long'. As idiosyncratically designed as the smooth- and long-haired versions, the Wire-haired Dachshund is an endearingly whiskery little creature and may be the result of a cross between the Smooth-haired Dachshund and a Dandie Dinmont Terrier or Schnauzer. Napoleon Bonaparte was a fond Dachshund owner.

Wire-haired Dachshund

This small and adorable dog is Sally's favourite.

Measurements
Length: 18cm (7in)
Height to top of head: 12cm (4¾in)

Materials
- Pair of 2¾mm (US 2) knitting needles
- Double-pointed 2¾mm (US 2) knitting needles (for holding stitches and for tail)
- 25g (1oz) of Rowan Fine Tweed in Keld 363 (ke)
- 15g (½oz) of Rowan Kidsilk Haze in Mud 652 (mu) used DOUBLE throughout
- NOTE: some parts of the dog use one strand of ke and one strand of mu held together, and this is called kem
- Small amount of Rowan Pure Wool 4ply in Eau de Nil 450 (en) for collar
- 2 pipecleaners for legs
- Tiny amount of Rowan Pure Wool 4ply in Black 404 (bl) for eyes and nose
- 2 tiny black beads for eyes and sewing needle and black thread for sewing on

Abbreviations
See page 172.
See page 172 for Colour Knitting.
See page 172 for I-cord Technique.
See page 172 for Wrap and Turn Method.
See page 172 for Loopy Stitch. Work 2-finger loopy stitch throughout this pattern.

Right Back Leg
With mu, cast on 11 sts.
Beg with a k row, work 2 rows st st.
Row 3: K3, k2tog, k1, k2tog, k3. *(9 sts)*
Row 4: Purl.
Row 5: K2, k2tog, k1, k2tog, k2. *(7 sts)*
Row 6: Purl.
Join in ke and cont in kem.
Row 7: Knit.
Row 8: Purl.
Row 9: Inc, k5, inc. *(9 sts)*
Row 10: Purl.
Row 11: Inc, k7, inc. *(11 sts)*
Row 12: Purl.*
Row 13: Cast (bind) off 5 sts, k to end (hold 6 sts on spare needle for Right Side of Body).

Left Back Leg
Work as for Right Back Leg to *.
Row 13: K6, cast (bind) off 5 sts (hold 6 sts on spare needle for Left Side of Body).

Right Front Leg
With mu, cast on 11 sts.
Beg with a k row, work 2 rows st st.
Row 3: K3, k2tog, k1, k2tog, k3. *(9 sts)*
Row 4: Purl.
Join in ke and cont in kem.
Row 5: K2, k2tog, k1, k2tog, k2. *(7 sts)*
Row 6: Purl.
Row 7: Inc, k5, inc. *(9 sts)*
Row 8: Purl.
Row 9: Inc, k7, inc. *(11 sts)*
Row 10: Purl.**
Row 11: Cast (bind) off 5 sts, k to end (hold 6 sts on spare needle for Right Side of Body).

Left Front Leg
Work as for Right Front Leg to **.
Row 11: K6, cast (bind) off 5 sts (hold 6 sts on spare needle for Left Side of Body).

Tail
Knit the i-cord tail firmly and you can then bend it into shape.

Right Side of Body

Row 1: With kem, cast on 2 sts, with RS facing k6 from spare needle of Right Front Leg, cast on 6 sts. *(14 sts)*

Row 2: Purl.

Row 3: Inc, k13, cast on 6 sts. *(21 sts)*

Row 4: Purl.

Row 5: Inc, k20, cast on 6 sts. *(28 sts)*

Row 6: Purl.

Row 7: Inc, k27, cast on 2 sts, with RS facing k6 from spare needle of Right Back Leg, cast on 1 st. *(38 sts)*

Work 5 rows st st.

Row 13: K36, k2tog. *(37 sts)*

Row 14: P2tog, p35. *(36 sts)*

Row 15: Knit.

Row 16: Cast (bind) off 7 sts, p27 icos, p2tog. *(28 sts)*

Row 17: K2tog, k8, cast (bind) off 18 sts (hold 9 sts on spare needle for right neck).

Left Side of Body

Row 1: With kem, cast on 2 sts, with WS facing p6 from spare needle of Left Front Leg, cast on 6 sts. *(14 sts)*

Row 2: Knit.

Row 3: Inc, p13, cast on 6 sts. *(21 sts)*

Row 4: Knit.

Row 5: Inc, p20, cast on 6 sts. *(28 sts)*

Row 6: Knit.

Row 7: Inc, p27, cast on 2 sts, with WS facing p6 from spare needle of Left Back Leg, cast on 1 st. *(38 sts)*

Work 5 rows st st.

Row 13: P36, p2tog. *(37 sts)*

Row 14: K2tog, k35. *(36 sts)*

Row 15: Purl.

Row 16: Cast (bind) off 7 sts, k27 icos, k2tog. *(28 sts)*

Row 17: P2tog, p8, cast (bind) off 18 sts (hold 9 sts on spare needle for left neck).

Head

Trim the eyebrows and leave the moustache long.

Neck and Head

Row 1: With kem and with RS facing, k9 held for neck from spare needle of Right Side of Body, then k9 held for neck from spare needle of Left Side of Body. *(18 sts)*

Row 2: P1, p2tog, p12, p2tog, p1. *(16 sts)*

Row 3: Knit.

Row 4: P1, p2tog, p10, p2tog, p1. *(14 sts)*

Row 5: K12, wrap and turn (leave 2 sts on left-hand needle unworked).

Row 6: Working top of head on centre 10 sts only, p10, w&t.

Row 7: K10, w&t.

Row 8: P10, w&t.

Row 9: K10, w&t.

Row 10: P10, w&t.

Row 11: Knit across all sts. *(14 sts in total)*

Row 12: Purl.

Row 13: K1, k2tog, k8, k2tog, k1. *(12 sts)*

Row 14: Purl.

Row 15: K10, w&t (leave 2 sts on left-hand needle unworked).

Row 16: Working top of head on centre 8 sts only p8, w&t.

Row 17: K8, w&t.

Row 18: P8, w&t.

Join in mu.

Row 19: K2kem, loopy st 3mu, k2kem, loopy st 3mu, k2kem. *(12 sts in total)*

Row 20: P1kem, [p2togmu] twice, p2kem, [p2togmu] twice, p1kem. *(8 sts)*

Row 21: K1kem, loopy st 2mu, k2kem, loopy st 2mu, k1kem.

Row 22: P1kem, p2mu, p2kem, p2mu, p1kem.

Row 23: K1kem, loopy st 2mu, k2kem, loopy st 2mu, k1kem.

Row 24: P8kem.

Cast (bind) off.

Tail

With two double-pointed needles and ke, cast on 1 st.

Work in i-cord as folls:

Knit 2 rows.

Row 3: Inc. *(2 sts)*

Knit 16 rows.

Row 20: K2tog and fasten off.

Tummy

With kem, cast on 7 sts.

Beg with a k row, work 52 rows st st.

Join in 2 ends mu.

Row 53: K2kem, k3mu, k2kem.

Row 54: P2kem, p3mu, p2kem.

Row 55: K1kem, k5mu, k1kem.

Row 56: P1kem, p5mu, p1kem.

Cont in mu.

Work 12 rows st st.

Row 69: K2tog, k3, k2tog. *(5 sts)*

Work 13 rows st st.

Row 83: K2tog, k1, k2tog. *(3 sts)*

Row 84: Purl.

Row 85: K3tog and fasten off.

Ear

(make 2 the same)

With ke, cast on 6 sts.

Beg with a k row, work 4 rows st st.

Row 5: K2tog, k2, k2tog. *(4 sts)*

Work 3 rows st st.

Cast (bind) off.

Collar

With en, cast on 26 sts.

Work one row.

Cast (bind) off.

To Make Up

See also diagram and notes on page 173.

SEWING IN ENDS Sew in ends, leaving ends from cast on and cast (bound) off rows for sewing up.

LEGS With WS together, fold leg in half. Starting at paw, sew up leg on RS using mu for paws and kem for legs.

BODY Sew along back of dog and around bottom.

HEAD Fold cast (bound) off row of head in half and sew 1cm (⅜in) down nose.

TUMMY Sew cast on row of tummy to bottom of dog's bottom (where back legs begin), and sew cast (bound) off row to chin. Ease and sew tummy to fit body. Leave a 2.5cm (1in) gap between front and back legs on one side.

STUFFING Pipecleaners are used to stiffen the legs and help bend them into shape. Fold a pipecleaner into a 'U' shape and measure against front two legs. Cut to approximately fit, leaving an extra 2.5cm (1in) at both ends. Fold these ends over to stop pipecleaner poking out of paws. Roll a little stuffing around pipecleaner and slip into body, one end down each front leg. Repeat with second pipecleaner and back legs. Starting at the head, stuff the dog firmly, then sew up the gap. Mould body into shape.

TAIL Sew cast (bound) off end of tail to dog where back meets bottom.

EARS Sew cast on row of each ear to side of dog's head, following natural slope of head and with 2 sts between ears.

EYEBROWS Trim loopy stitches to approx 7mm (¼in).

EYES With bl, sew 2-loop French knots just below eyebrows. Sew beads on top of French knots.

MOUSTACHE Trim loopy stitches to approx 3cm (1¼in).

NOSE With bl, embroider nose in satin stitch.

COLLAR Sew ends of collar together and pop over head.

Chinese Crested Dog

One of the oddest-looking breeds, but loyal and loving, the Chinese Crested comes in two varieties, Powder Puff and hairless. Ours is the hairless version with no fur at all on the body, though they do have a sort of Warhol-like wig arrangement on their heads and what look like hairy flares, slightly reminiscent of Agnetha from ABBA. Sam the Chinese Crested won the World's Ugliest Dog Contest from 2003 to 2005. Like many dogs their origins are hazy, but Chinese Cresteds almost certainly don't originate from China.

Chinese Crested Dog

An extraordinary and unique lapdog, made using loopy stitch and Fair Isle.

Measurements

Length: 10cm (4in)
Height to top of ears : 14cm (5½in)

Materials

- Pair of 2¾mm (US2) knitting needles
- Double-pointed 2¾mm (US 2) knitting needles (for holding stitches)
- 20g (¾oz) of Rowan Pure Wool 4ply in Mocha 417 (mo)
- 10g (¼oz) of Rowan Kidsilk Haze in Cream 634 (cr) used DOUBLE throughout
- 10g (¼oz) of Rowan Cashsoft 4ply in Pretty 460 (pr)
- 3 pipecleaners for legs and tail
- Tiny amount of Rowan Pure Wool 4ply in Black 404 (bl) for eyes and nose

Abbreviations

See page 172.
See page 172 for Colour Knitting.
See page 172 for Wrap and Turn Method.
See page 172 for Loopy Stitch. Work 2-finger loopy stitch throughout this pattern.

Right Back Leg

With mo, cast on 7 sts.
Beg with a k row, work 4 rows st st.
Row 5: K2tog, inc, k1, inc, k2tog. *(7 sts)*
Work 3 rows st st.
Rep last 4 rows once more.
Row 13: K2tog, inc, k1, inc, k2tog. *(7 sts)*
Row 14: Purl.
Join in cr.
Row 15: K1mo, loopy st 5cr, k1mo.
Break cr.
Row 16: Inc, p5, inc. *(9 sts)*
Row 17: K2tog, [inc] twice, k1, [inc] twice, k2tog. *(11 sts)*
Row 18: Inc, p9, inc. *(13 sts)*
Row 19: Inc, k11, inc. *(15 sts)*
Row 20: Purl.
Row 21: Inc, k13, inc. *(17 sts)*
Row 22: Purl.
Row 23: Inc, k15, inc. *(19 sts)*
Row 24: Purl.*
Row 25: Cast (bind) off 10 sts, k to end (hold 9 sts on spare needle for Right Side of Body).

Left Back Leg

Work as for Right Back Leg to *.
Row 25: K9, cast (bind) off 10 sts (hold 9 sts on spare needle for Left Side of Body).

Right Front Leg

With mo, cast on 7 sts.
Beg with a k row, work 4 rows st st.
Row 5: K2tog, inc, k1, inc, k2tog. *(7 sts)*
Work 3 rows st st.
Rep last 4 rows once more.
Row 13: K2tog, inc, k1, inc, k2tog. *(7 sts)*
Row 14: Purl.
Join in cr.
Row 15: K1mo, loopy st 5cr, k1mo.
Break cr.
Row 16: Purl.
Row 17: Inc, k5, inc. *(9 sts)*
Work 3 rows st st.
Row 21: Inc, k7, inc. *(11 sts)*

Row 22: Purl.**
Row 23: Cast (bind) off 6 sts, k to end (hold 5 sts on spare needle for Right Side of Body).

Left Front Leg

Work as for Right Front Leg to **.
Row 23: K5, cast (bind) off 6 sts (hold 5 sts on spare needle for Left Side of Body).

Right Side of Body

Row 1: With mo, cast on 1 st, with RS facing k5 from spare needle of Right Front Leg, cast on 5 sts. *(11 sts)*
Row 2: Purl.
Row 3: K11, cast on 5 sts. *(16 sts)*
Row 4: Purl.
Row 5: K16, cast on 5 sts, with RS facing k9 from spare needle of Right Back Leg. *(30 sts)*
Row 6: Purl.
Row 7: Inc, k29. *(31 sts)*
Join in pr.
Row 8: P30mo, p1pr.
Row 9: K2pr, k2mo, k1pr, k26mo.
Row 10: P25mo, p2pr, p2mo, p2pr.
Row 11: K6pr, k25mo.
Row 12: P25mo, p2pr, p1mo, p3pr.
Row 13: K5pr, k26mo.
Row 14: P2togmo, p24mo, p2pr, p2mo, p1pr. *(30 sts)*
Row 15: K4pr, k26mo. *(30 sts)*
Row 16: P27mo, p3pr.
Row 17: K8mo, cast (bind) off 22 sts mo (hold 8 sts on spare needle for right neck).

Left Side of Body

Row 1: With mo, cast on 1 st, with WS facing p5 from spare needle of Left Front Leg, cast on 5 sts. *(11 sts)*
Row 2: Knit.
Row 3: P11, cast on 5 sts. *(16 sts)*
Row 4: Knit.
Row 5: P16, cast on 5 sts, with WS facing p9 from spare needle of Left Back Leg. *(30 sts)*
Row 6: Knit.

Row 7: Inc, p29. *(31 sts)*
Join in pr.
Row 8: K30mo, k1pr.
Row 9: P2pr, p2mo, p1pr, p26mo.
Row 10: K25mo, k2pr, k2mo, k2pr.
Row 11: P6pr, p25mo.
Row 12: K25mo, k2pr, k1mo, k3pr.
Row 13: P5pr, p26mo.
Row 14: K2togmo, k24mo, k2pr, k2mo, k1pr. *(30 sts)*
Row 15: P4pr, p26mo. *(30 sts)*
Row 16: K27mo, k3pr.
Row 17: P8mo, cast (bind) off 22 sts mo (hold 8 sts on spare needle for left neck).

Neck and Head

Row 1: With mo and with RS facing, k8 held for neck from spare needle of Right Side of Body, then k8 held for neck from spare needle of Left Side of Body. *(16 sts)*
Row 2: P7, p2tog, p7. *(15 sts)*
Row 3: Knit.
Row 4: P1, p2tog, p9, p2tog, p1. *(13 sts)*
Row 5: Knit.
Row 6: Purl.
Row 7: K11, wrap and turn (leave 2 sts on left-hand needle unworked).
Row 8: Working top of head on centre 9 sts only, p9, w&t.
Row 9: K9, w&t.
Row 10: P9, w&t.
Join in cr.
Row 11: K2mo, loopy st 5cr, k4mo. *(13 sts in total)*
Row 12: Purl in mo.
Row 13: K4mo, loopy st 5cr, k2mo, w&t (leave 2 sts on left-hand needle unworked).
Break cr.
Row 14: Working top of head on centre 9 sts only, p9, w&t.
Row 15: K9, w&t.
Row 16: P9, w&t.
Row 17: Knit across all sts. *(13 sts in total)*
Join in pr.

Row 18: P2mo, p3pr, p1mo, p2pr, p1mo, p2mo. *(11 sts)*
Row 19: K1mo, k2togmo, k3pr, k2mo, k2togmo, k1mo. *(9 sts)*
Row 20: P2mo, p3pr, p1mo, p2pr, p1mo.
Row 21: K1mo, k2togmo, k2pr, k1mo, k2togmo, k1mo. *(7 sts)*
Row 22: P1mo, p2pr, p1mo, p2pr, p1mo.
Cont in pr.
Row 23: K3tog, k1, k3tog. *(3 sts)*
Row 24: P3tog and fasten off.

Tail

With mo, cast on 5 sts.
Beg with a k row, work 12 rows st st.
Join in cr.
Row 13: K1mo, loopy st 3cr, k1mo.
Row 14: Purl in mo.
Rep rows 13–14, 5 times more.
Row 25: K2togmo, loopy st 1cr, k2togmo. *(3 sts)*
Break cr.
Row 26: Purl.
Row 27: K3tog and fasten off.

Body
Use Fair Isle for the Chinese Crested's hairless tummy.

Tail

The tail loops need to be long for added luxury.

Tummy

With mo, cast on 1 st.
Row 1: Inc. *(2 sts)*
Row 2: Purl.
Row 3: [Inc] twice. *(4 sts)*
Row 4: Purl.
Row 5: Inc, k2, inc. *(6 sts)*
Row 6: Purl.
Row 7: Inc, k4, inc. *(8 sts)*
Row 8: Purl.
Work 8 rows st st.
Join in pr.
Row 17: K1pr, k2mo, k3pr, k1mo, k1pr.
Row 18: P3pr, p1mo, p2pr, p2mo.
Row 19: K2mo, k3pr, k1mo, k2pr.
Row 20: P8pr.
Row 21: K3pr, k2mo, k2pr, k1mo.
Row 22: P2mo, p1pr, p2mo, p3pr.
Row 23: K2mo, k6pr.
Row 24: P8pr.
Row 25: K3pr, k1mo, k2pr, k2mo.
Row 26: P2mo, p6pr.
Row 27: K8pr.
Row 28: P8pr.
Row 29: K1pr, k2mo, k1pr, k2mo, k2pr.
Row 30: P2pr, p2mo, p1pr, p2mo, p1pr.
Row 31: K8pr.
Row 32: P8pr.
Row 33: K2pr, k1mo, k1pr, k2mo, k2pr.
Row 34: P8pr.
Row 35: K6pr, k2mo.
Row 36: P3mo, p2pr, p1mo, p2pr.
Row 37: K3pr, k2mo, k1pr, k2mo.
Row 38: P4mo, p2pr, p1mo, p1pr.
Row 39: K2mo, k3pr, k3mo.
Row 40: P2mo, p2pr, p1mo, p1pr, p2mo.
Row 41: K1mo, k3pr, k1mo, k1pr, k1mo.
Row 42: P1mo, p4pr, p2mo, p1pr.
Row 43: K2togpr, k2pr, k2mo, k2togpr. *(6 sts)*
Row 44: P6pr.
Row 45: K6pr.
Row 46: P2mo, p4pr.
Row 47: K2pr, k2mo, k2pr.

Row 48: P2pr, p2mo, p1pr, p1mo.
Row 49: K2mo, k4pr.
Row 50: P6pr.
Row 51: K2togmo, k2pr, k2togpr. *(4 sts)*
Row 52: P4pr.
Row 53: K3mo, k1pr.
Row 54: P4pr.
Row 55: K4pr.
Row 56: P2pr, p2mo.
Row 57: K2mo, k2pr.
Row 58: P3pr, p1mo.
Row 59: K1mo, k3pr.
Cont in pr.
Work 4 rows st st.
Row 64: [K2tog] twice. *(2 sts)*
Row 65: P2tog and fasten off.

Right Ear

With mo, cast on 7 sts.
Beg with a k row, work 6 rows st st.
Row 7: K2tog, k3, k2tog. *(5 sts)*
Row 8: Purl.
Join in cr.
Row 9: Loopy st 1cr, k4mo.
Row 10: Purl in mo.
Row 11: Loopy st 1cr, k4mo.
Row 12: P2togmo, p1mo, p2togmo. *(3 sts)*
Row 13: Loopy st 1cr, k2mo.
Break cr.
Row 14: P3tog and fasten off.

Left Ear

With mo, cast on 7 sts.
Beg with a k row, work 6 rows st st.
Row 7: K2tog, k3, k2tog. *(5 sts)*
Row 8: Purl.
Join in cr.
Row 9: K4mo, loopy st 1cr.
Row 10: Purl in mo.
Row 11: K4mo, loopy st 1cr.
Row 12: P2togmo, p1mo, p2togmo. *(3 sts)*
Row 13: K2mo, loopy st 1cr.
Break cr.
Row 14: P3tog and fasten off.

To Make Up

See also diagram and notes on page 173.

SEWING IN ENDS Sew in ends, leaving ends from cast on and cast (bound) off rows for sewing up.

LEGS With WS together, fold leg in half. Starting at paw, sew up leg on RS.

BODY Sew along back of dog and around bottom.

TUMMY Sew cast on row of tummy to top of dog's bottom (where back meets top of bottom), and sew cast (bound) off row to chin. Ease and sew tummy to fit body. Leave a 2.5cm (1in) gap between front and back legs on one side.

STUFFING Pipecleaners are used to stiffen the legs and help bend them into shape. Fold a pipecleaner into a 'U' shape and measure against front two legs. Cut to approximately fit, leaving an extra 2.5cm (1in) at both ends. Fold these ends over to stop pipecleaner poking out of paws. Roll a little stuffing around pipecleaner and slip into body, one end down each front leg. Repeat with second pipecleaner and back legs. Starting at the head, stuff the dog firmly, then sew up the gap. Mould body into shape.

TAIL Cut a pipecleaner 2.5cm (1in) longer than tail. Roll a little stuffing around pipecleaner, wrap tail around pipecleaner and sew up tail on RS. Push protruding pipecleaner end into dog where back meets bottom and sew tail on.

EARS Sew cast on row of each ear to side of dog's head, right ear on right side and left ear on left side, with 2 sts between ears and with wrong side of ears facing forwards. When sewing on ears, you can also sew down loopy stitch fringe to keep it down.

EYES With bl, sew 2-loop French knots positioned as in photograph.

NOSE With bl, embroider nose in satin stitch.

Cavalier King Charles Spaniel

Historically a lapdog, the charming Cavalier is much smaller than its spaniel relatives and was possibly originally crossed with a Pug to create its snub nose. Hugely popular, they were loved by Charles I and Charles II, and by Mary Queen of Scots who was beheaded with her little dog under her skirt: the dog reputedly died of grief a few days later. The Cavalier was the model of the pottery dogs, often seen in pairs, made by the Royal Staffordshire Pottery. The first Duke of Marlborough owned Cavaliers and the colouring of this dog is named in honour of him and his estate, Blenheim.

Cavalier King Charles Spaniel

This is a rewarding dog to knit and a good introduction to loopy stitch and intarsia.

Measurements

Length: 15cm (6in)
Height to top of head: 13cm (5¼in)

Materials

- Pair of 2¾mm (US 2) knitting needles
- Double-pointed 2¾mm (US 2) knitting needles (for holding stitches and for tail)
- 15g (½oz) of Rowan Pure Wool 4ply in Snow 412 (sn)
- 10g (¼oz) of Rowan Pure Wool 4ply in Mocha 417 (mo)
- Small amount of Rowan Pure Wool 4ply in Raspberry 428 (ra) for collar
- 2 pipecleaners for legs
- Tiny amount of Rowan Pure Wool 4ply in Black 404 (bl) for eyes and nose

Abbreviations

See page 172.
See page 172 for Colour Knitting.
See page 172 for I-cord Technique.
See page 172 for Wrap and Turn Method.
See page 172 for Loopy Stitch. Work 2-finger loopy stitch throughout this pattern.

Right Back Leg

With sn, cast on 11 sts.
Beg with a k row, work 2 rows st st.
Row 3: Inc, k2, k2tog, k1, k2tog, k2, inc. *(11 sts)*
Row 4: Purl.
Row 5: Inc, [k2tog] twice, k1, [k2tog] twice, inc. *(9 sts)*
Work 7 rows st st, working loopy st on 2nd st and 2nd-to-last st on every k row for rest of leg.*
Row 13: Inc, k2, inc, k1, inc, k2, inc. *(13 sts)*
Row 14: Purl.
Row 15: K2tog, [k1, inc] 4 times, k1, k2tog. *(15 sts)*
Row 16: Purl.
Row 17: K6, inc, k1, inc, k6. *(17 sts)*
Row 18: Purl.
Row 19: K7, inc, k1, inc, k7. *(19 sts)*
Row 20: Purl.
Row 21: K8, inc, k1, inc, k8. *(21 sts)*
Row 22: Purl.**
Row 23: Cast (bind) off 10 sts, k to end (hold 11 sts on spare needle for Right Side of Body).

Left Back Leg

Work as for Right Back Leg to **.
Row 23: K11, cast (bind) off 10 sts (hold 11 sts on spare needle for Left Side of Body).

Right Front Leg

Work as for Right Back Leg to *.
Row 13: Inc, k7, inc. *(11 sts)*
Work 3 rows st st.
Row 17: Inc, k9, inc. *(13 sts)*
Row 18: Purl.***
Row 19: Cast (bind) off 6 sts, k to end (hold 7 sts on spare needle for Right Side of Body).

Left Front Leg

Work as for Right Front Leg to ***.
Row 19: K7, cast (bind) off 6 sts (hold 7 sts on spare needle for Left Side of Body).

Right Side of Body

Row 1: With sn and mo, cast on 1 st sn, with RS facing k7sn from spare needle of Right Front Leg, cast on 5 sts mo. *(13 sts)*
Row 2: P5mo, p7sn, incsn. *(14 sts)*
Row 3: Incsn, k8sn, k5mo, cast on 5 sts mo. *(20 sts)*
Row 4: P9mo, p11sn.
Row 5: K11sn, k9mo, cast on 4 sts mo, with RS facing k3mo, k2sn, k6mo from spare needle of Right Back Leg, cast on 1 st mo. *(36 sts)*
Row 6: P7mo, p2sn, p15mo, p11sn, incsn. *(37 sts)*
Row 7: K13sn, k16mo, k1sn, k7mo.
Row 8: P6mo, p2sn, p16mo, p13sn.
Row 9: K14sn, k1mo, k1sn, k14mo, k1sn, k6mo.
Row 10: P21mo, p16sn.
Row 11: K16sn, k21mo.
Row 12: P20mo, p9sn, p4mo, p4sn.
Row 13: K1sn, k9mo, k7sn, k20mo.
Row 14: P9mo, p2sn, p3mo, p1sn, p4mo, p7sn, p10mo, p1sn.
Row 15: K3sn, k9mo, k7sn, k2mo, k3sn, k2mo, k3sn, k8mo.
Row 16: P7mo, p3sn, p3mo, p11sn, p8mo, p5sn.
Row 17: K7sn, k6mo, k11sn, k4mo, k3sn, k4mo, k2togmo. *(36 sts)*
Row 18: P2togmo, p3mo, p2sn, p4mo, p12sn, p4mo, p9sn. *(35 sts)*
Row 19: K10sn, k2mo, k15sn, k6mo, k2togmo. *(34 sts)*
Row 20: Cast (bind) off 7 sts mo and 10 sts sn, p17sn icos. *(17 sts)*
Row 21: K11sn (hold 11 sts on spare needle for right neck), cast (bind) off 6 sts sn.

Left Side of Body

Row 1: With sn and mo, cast on 1 st sn, with WS facing p7sn from spare needle of Left Front Leg, cast on 5 sts mo. *(13 sts)*
Row 2: K5mo, k7sn, incsn. *(14 sts)*

Head

To create the characteristic snub nose, make sure the muzzle is well stuffed.

Row 3: Incsn, p8sn, p5mo, cast on 5 sts mo. *(20 sts)*
Row 4: K9mo, k11sn.
Row 5: P11sn, p9mo, cast on 4 sts mo, with WS facing p3mo, p2sn, p6mo from spare needle of Left Back Leg, cast on 1 st mo. *(36 sts)*
Row 6: K7mo, k2sn, k15mo, k11sn, incsn. *(37 sts)*
Row 7: P13sn, p16mo, p1sn, p7mo.
Row 8: K6mo, k2sn, k16mo, k13sn.
Row 9: P14sn, p1mo, p1sn, p14mo, p1sn, p6mo.

Row 10: K21mo, k16sn.
Row 11: P16sn, p21mo.
Row 12: K20mo, k9sn, k4mo, k4sn.
Row 13: P1sn, p9mo, p7sn, p20mo.
Row 14: K9mo, k2sn, k3mo, k1sn, k4mo, k7sn, k10mo, k1sn.
Row 15: P3sn, p9mo, p7sn, p2mo, p3sn, p2mo, p3sn, p8mo.
Row 16: K7mo, k3sn, k3mo, k11sn, k8mo, k5sn.
Row 17: P7sn, p6mo, p11sn, p4mo, p3sn, p4mo, p2togmo. *(36 sts)*
Row 18: K2togmo, k3mo, k2sn, k4mo, k12sn, k4mo, k9sn. *(35 sts)*
Row 19: P10sn, p2mo, p15sn, p6mo, p2togmo. *(34 sts)*
Row 20: Cast (bind) off 7 sts mo and 10 sts sn, k17sn icos. *(17 sts)*
Row 21: P11sn (hold 11 sts on spare needle for left neck), cast (bind) off 6 sts sn.

Neck and Head

Row 1: With sn and with RS facing, k11 from spare needle of Right Side of Body, then k11 from spare needle of Left Side of Body. *(22 sts)*
Row 2: P5, p2tog, p8, p2tog, p5. *(20 sts)*
Row 3: K5, k2tog, k6, k2tog, k5. *(18 sts)*
Row 4: Inc, p16, inc. *(20 sts)*
Join in mo.
Row 5: K4sn, k2mo, k8sn, k2mo, k1sn, wrap and turn (leave 3 sts on left-hand needle unworked).
Row 6: Working top of head on centre 14 sts only, p1sn, p2mo, p8sn, p2mo, p1sn, w&t.
Row 7: K1sn, k3mo, k6sn, k3mo, k1sn, w&t.
Row 8: P1sn, p3mo, p6sn, p3mo, p1sn, w&t.
Row 9: K5mo, k4sn, k5mo, w&t.
Row 10: P5mo, p4sn, p5mo, w&t.
Row 11: K5mo, k4sn, k5mo, k3sn. *(20 sts in total)*
Row 12: P2sn, p6mo, p4sn, p6mo, p2sn.
Row 13: K2sn, k5mo, k6sn, k4mo, w&t (leave 3 sts on left-hand needle unworked).

Row 14: Working top of head on centre 14 sts only, p4mo, p6sn, p4mo, w&t.
Row 15: K5mo, k4sn, k5mo, w&t.
Row 16: P5mo, p4sn, p5mo, w&t.
Row 17: K6mo, k2sn, k6mo, w&t.
Row 18: P6mo, p2sn, p6mo, w&t.
Row 19: K5mo, k4sn, k5mo, k3sn. *(20 sts in total)*
Cont in sn.
Row 20: P3, p2tog, p4, p2tog, p4, p2tog, p3. *(17 sts)*
Row 21: K3, [k2tog] twice, k3, [k2tog] twice, k3. *(13 sts)*
Work 2 rows st st.
Row 24: P2tog, p9, p2tog. *(11 sts)*
Row 25: Knit.
Row 26: P2tog, p7, p2tog. *(9 sts)*
Cast (bind) off.

Tail

With two double-pointed needles and mo, cast on 8 sts.
Work i-cord as folls:
Knit 2 rows.
Row 3: K1, loopy st 1, k4, loopy st 1, k1.
Knit 2 rows.
Rep last 3 rows twice more.
Row 12: K1, loopy st 1, k4, loopy st 1, k1.
Join in sn.
Row 13: K3mo, k2sn, k3mo.
Row 14: K2mo, k4sn, k2mo.
Row 15: K1mo, loopy st 1sn, k4sn, loopy st 1sn, k1mo.
Cont in sn.
Knit 2 rows.
Row 18: K1, loopy st 1, k4, loopy st 1, k1.
Rep last 3 rows twice more.
Row 25: K2tog, k4, k2tog. *(6 sts)*
Knit one row.
Row 27: K1, loopy st 1, k2, loopy st 1, k1.
Row 28: K2tog, k2, k2tog. *(4 sts)*
Row 29: [K2tog] twice. *(2 sts)*
Row 30: K2tog and fasten off.

Tummy

With sn, cast on 6 sts.
Beg with a k row, work 2 rows st st.
Row 3: K2tog, k2, k2tog. *(4 sts)*
Work 13 rows st st.
Row 17: Inc, k2, inc. *(6 sts)*
Row 18: Purl.
Row 19: K1, loopy st 1, k2, loopy st 1, k1.
Row 20: Purl.
Rep rows 19–20, 11 times more.
Row 43: K2tog, k2, k2tog. *(4 sts)*
Work 4 rows st st.
Row 48: Inc, p2, inc. *(6 sts)*
Work 2 rows st st.
Row 51: K1, loopy st 1, k2, loopy st 1, k1.
Work 3 rows st st.
Rep last 4 rows 4 times more.
Work 6 rows st st.
Row 77: K2tog, k2, k2tog. *(4 sts)*
Work 7 rows st st.
Row 85: [K2tog] twice. *(2 sts)*
Row 86: P2tog and fasten off.

Ear

(make 2 the same)
With mo, cast on 4 sts.
Beg with a k row, work 2 rows st st.
Row 3: Inc, loopy st 2, inc. *(6 sts)*
Row 4: Purl.
Row 5: Inc, loopy st 4, inc. *(8 sts)*
Row 6: Purl.
Row 7: K1, loopy st 6, k1.
Row 8: Purl.
Repeat rows 7–8, 4 times more.
Row 17: K2tog, loopy st 4, k2tog. *(6 sts)*
Cast (bind) off.

Collar

With ra, cast on 26 sts.
Knit one row.
Cast (bind) off.

Tail

Manipulate the tail so that it curves gently.

To Make Up

See also diagram and notes on page 173.

SEWING IN ENDS Sew in ends, leaving ends from cast on and cast (bound) off rows for sewing up.

LEGS With WS together, fold leg in half. Starting at paw, sew up leg on RS.

BODY Sew along back of dog and around bottom.

HEAD Fold cast (bound) off row of head in half and sew from nose to chin.

TUMMY Sew cast on row of tummy to bottom of dog's bottom (where back legs begin), and sew cast (bound) off row to chin. Ease and sew tummy to fit body. Leave a 2.5cm (1in) gap between front and back legs on one side.

STUFFING Pipecleaners are used to stiffen the legs and help bend them into shape. Fold a pipecleaner into a 'U' shape and measure against front two legs. Cut to approximately fit, leaving an extra 2.5cm (1in) at both ends. Fold these ends over to stop pipecleaner poking out of paws. Roll a little stuffing around pipecleaner and slip into body, one end down each front leg. Repeat with second pipecleaner and back legs. Starting at the head, stuff the dog firmly, then sew up the gap. Mould body into shape.

TAIL Sew cast (bound) off end of tail to dog where back meets bottom, with loops on underside.

EARS Sew cast on row of each ear to side of dog's head, following natural slope of head and with 4 sts between ears.

EYES With bl, sew 2-loop French knots positioned as in photograph.

NOSE With bl, embroider nose in satin stitch.

COLLAR Sew ends of collar together and pop over head.

Utility

Hungarian Puli

The amazingly dreadlocked Puli (plural Pulik), although impractical-looking is in fact bred as a working dog. Pulik work in tandem with the larger, fiercer Komondor, herding and guarding sheep; both breeds have corded coats that are difficult for wolves to penetrate. The Puli was brought to Hungary by the Magyars during the Mongol invasion. Mark Zuckerberg has a Puli called Beast, who has his own Facebook account.

Hungarian Puli

Loops, loops and more loops...for advanced knitters.

Measurements
Length: 17cm (6¾in)
Height to top of head: 14cm (5½in)

Materials
- Pair of 2¾mm (US 2) knitting needles
- Double-pointed 2¾mm (US 2) knitting needles (for holding stitches)
- 40g (1½oz) of Rowan Fine Tweed in Pendle 377 (pe)
- Tiny amount of Rowan Cashsoft 4ply in Pretty 460 (pr) for tongue
- Small amount of Rowan Cashsoft 4ply in Quartz 446 (qu) for collar
- 3 pipecleaners for legs and tail

Abbreviations
See page 172.
See page 172 for Wrap and Turn Method.
See page 172 for Loopy Stitch. Work 3-finger loopy stitch throughout this pattern.
NOTE: this dog has no ears.

Right Back Leg
With pe, cast on 11 sts.
Beg with a k row, work 2 rows st st.
Row 3: Inc, k2, k2tog, k1, k2tog, k2, inc. *(11 sts)*
Row 4: Purl.
Row 5: Inc, [k2tog] twice, k1, [k2tog] twice, inc. *(9 sts)*
Work 7 rows st st.
Row 13: K1, loopy st 7, k1.
Row 14 and every alt row: Purl.
Row 15: Inc, loopy st 7, inc. *(11 sts)*
Row 17: Inc, loopy st 9, inc. *(13 sts)*
Row 19: Inc, loopy st 11, inc.* *(15 sts)*
Row 21: Inc, loopy st 13, inc. *(17 sts)*
Row 23: Inc, loopy st 15, inc.** *(19 sts)*
Row 25: Cast (bind) off 9 sts, k to end (hold 10 sts on spare needle for Right Side of Body).

Left Back Leg
Work as for Right Back Leg to **.
Row 24: Purl.
Row 25: K10, cast (bind) off 9 sts (hold 10 sts on spare needle for Left Side of Body).

Right Front Leg
Work as for Right Back Leg to *.
Row 20: Purl.
Row 21: K1, loopy st 13, k1.
Row 22: Purl.***
Row 23: Cast (bind) off 7 sts, k to end (hold 8 sts on spare needle for Right Side of Body).

Left Front Leg
Work as for Right Front Leg to ***.
Row 23: K8, cast (bind) off 7 sts (hold 8 sts on spare needle for Left Side of Body).

Shaping

Don't worry if you make mistakes as the loopy stitch will hide most errors.

Right Side of Body

Row 1: With pe, cast on 1 st, with RS facing k8 from spare needle of Right Front Leg, cast on 5 sts. *(14 sts)*

Row 2: Purl.

Row 3: Inc, k13, cast on 4 sts. *(19 sts)*

Row 4: Purl.

Row 5: K1, loopy st 18, cast on 4 sts, with RS facing loopy st 10 from spare needle of Right Back Leg. *(33 sts)*

Row 6: Purl.

Row 7: K1, loopy st 31, k1.

Row 8: Purl.

Rep rows 7–8, 4 times more.

Row 17: K11 (hold 11 sts on spare needle for right neck), cast (bind) off 22 sts.

Left Side of Body

Row 1: With pe, cast on 1 st, with WS facing p8 from spare needle of Left Front Leg, cast on 5 sts. *(14 sts)*

Row 2: Knit.

Row 3: Inc, p13, cast on 4 sts. *(19 sts)*

Row 4: K1, loopy st 17, k1.

Row 5: P19, cast on 4 sts, with WS facing p10 from spare needle of Left Back Leg. *(33 sts)*

Row 6: K1, loopy st 31, k1. *(33 sts)*

Row 7: Purl.

Row 8: K1, loopy st 31, k1.

Rep rows 7–8, 4 times more.

Row 17: P11 (hold 11 sts on spare needle for left neck), cast (bind) off 22 sts.

Neck and Head

Row 1: With pe and with RS facing, k11 from spare needle of Right Side of Body, then k11 from spare needle of Left Side of Body. *(22 sts)*

Row 2: P5, p2tog, p8, p2tog, p5. *(20 sts)*

Row 3: K1, loopy st 18, k1.

Row 4: Purl.

Row 5: K17, wrap and turn (leave 3 sts on left-hand needle unworked).

Row 6: Working top of head on centre 14 sts only, p14, w&t.

Row 7: Loopy st 14, w&t.

Row 8: P14, w&t.

Row 9: K14, w&t.

Row 10: P14, w&t.

Row 11: Loopy st 14, k3. *(20 sts in total)*

Row 12: Purl.

Row 13: K17, w&t (leave 3 sts on left-hand needle unworked).

Row 14: Working top of head on centre 14 sts only, p14, w&t.

Row 15: Loopy st 14, w&t.

Row 16: P14, w&t.

Row 17: K14, w&t.

Row 18: P14, w&t.

Row 19: Loopy st 14, k3. *(20 sts in total)*

Body

When sewing up, try not to catch the loops in the seams.

Row 20: P3, p2tog, p4, p2tog, p4, p2tog, p3. *(17 sts)*
Row 21: K3, [k2tog] twice, k3, [k2tog] twice, k3. *(13 sts)*
Row 22: Purl.
Row 23: K1, loopy st 11, k1.
Row 24: P2tog, p9, p2tog. *(11 sts)*
Row 25: Knit.
Row 26: P2tog, p7, p2tog. *(9 sts)*
Cast (bind) off.

Tail

With pe, cast on 8 sts.
Work 2 rows st st.
Row 3: K1, loopy st 6, k1.
Row 4: Purl.
Rep rows 3–4, 4 times more.
Cast (bind) off.

Tummy

With pe, cast on 5 sts.
Beg with k row, work 48 rows st st.
Cast (bind) off.

Tongue

With pr, cast on 3 sts.
Knit one row.
Cast (bind) off.

Collar

With qu, cast on 24 sts.
Knit one row.
Cast (bind) off.

To Make Up

See also diagram and notes on page 173.

SEWING IN ENDS Sew in ends, leaving ends from cast on and cast (bound) off rows for sewing up.

LEGS With WS together, fold leg in half. Starting at paw, sew up leg on RS.

BODY Sew along back of dog and around bottom.

HEAD Fold cast (bound) off row of head in half and sew from nose to chin.

TUMMY Sew cast on row of tummy to bottom of dog's bottom (where back legs begin), and sew cast (bound) off row to chin. Ease and sew tummy to fit body. Leave a 2.5cm (1in) gap between front and back legs on one side.

STUFFING Pipecleaners are used to stiffen the legs and help bend them into shape. Fold a pipecleaner into a 'U' shape and measure against front two legs. Cut to approximately fit, leaving an extra 2.5cm (1in) at both ends. Fold these ends over to stop pipecleaner poking out of paws. Roll a little stuffing around pipecleaner and slip into body, one end down each front leg. Repeat with second pipecleaner and back legs. Starting at the head, stuff the dog firmly, then sew up the gap. Mould body into shape.

TAIL Cut a pipecleaner 2.5cm (1in) longer than tail. Roll a little stuffing around pipecleaner, wrap tail around pipecleaner and sew up tail on RS. Push protruding pipecleaner end into dog where back meets bottom, sew tail on and bend over in to characteristic shape.

TONGUE Sew on tongue approx 2cm (¾in) below tip of nose.

COLLAR Sew ends of collar together and pop over head.

Shar Pei

Originally from China, the Shar Pei can be excessively wrinkly, or just a bit wrinkly like ours. The wrinkles are useful in a fight; if their opponent has a mouthful of their skin, it's loose enough for them to turn around and attack back. The Shar Pei almost disappeared during the Cultural Revolution, due to a huge dog tax and ban on all breeding, and they were also considered something of a delicacy. In 1973 Matgo Law, a Hong Kong breeder, appealed in a dog magazine to save the breed and around 200 were smuggled to America. This timely intervention has ensured the breed's survival.

Shar Pei

The Shar Pei has wrinkly skin and you can, if you like, add more wrinkles to your dog.

Measurements
Length: 18cm (7in)
Height to top of head: 14cm (5½in)

Materials
- Pair of 2¾mm (US 2) knitting needles
- Double-pointed 2¾mm (US 2) knitting needles (for holding stitches)
- 30g (1¼oz) of Rowan Pure Wool 4ply in Toffee 453 (to)
- 5g (⅙oz) of Rowan Pure Wool 4ply in Mocha 417 (mo)
- Small amount of Rowan Cashsoft 4ply in Toxic 459 (tx) for collar
- 3 pipecleaners for legs and tail
- Tiny amount of Rowan Pure Wool 4ply in Black 404 (bl) for eyes and nose

Abbreviations
See page 172.
See page 172 for Colour Knitting.
See page 172 for Wrap and Turn Method.

Right Back Leg
With to, cast on 6 sts.
Beg with a k row, work 2 rows st st.
Row 3: Inc, k1, k2tog, k1, inc. *(7 sts)*
Row 4: Purl.
Row 5: Inc, k2tog, k1, k2tog, inc. *(7 sts)*
Work 9 rows st st.
Row 15: K2tog, inc, k1, inc, k2tog. *(7 sts)*
Row 16: Purl.
Row 17: K1, inc, k3, inc, k1. *(9 sts)*
Row 18: Purl.
Row 19: K1, inc, k5, inc, k1. *(11 sts)*
Row 20: Purl.
Row 21: K1, inc, k7, inc, k1. *(13 sts)*
Row 22: Purl.
Row 23: K1, inc, k4, inc, k4, inc, k1. *(16 sts)*
Row 24: Purl.
Row 25: K1, inc, k12, inc, k1. *(18 sts)*
Row 26: Purl.
Work 5 rows st st.
Row 32: To make a wrinkle, *pick up st from row 26, p2tog (st on needle and st picked up), p1, rep from * to end of row.**
Row 33: Cast (bind) off 9 sts, k to end (hold 9 sts on spare needle for Right Side of Body).

Left Back Leg
Work as for Right Back Leg to **.
Row 33: K9, cast (bind) off 9 sts (hold 9 sts on spare needle for Left Side of Body).

Right Front Leg
With to, cast on 6 sts.
Beg with a k row, work 2 rows st st.
Row 3: Inc, [k2tog] twice, inc. *(6 sts)*
Row 4: Purl.
Row 5: K2, [inc] twice, k2. *(8 sts)*
Work 7 rows st st.
Row 13: K1, inc, k4, inc, k1. *(10 sts)*
Row 14: Purl.
Work 2 rows st st.
Row 17: K1, inc, k6, inc, k1. *(12 sts)*
Row 18: Purl.
Row 19: K1, inc, k8, inc, k1. *(14 sts)*

Body
For more wrinkles, add an extra six rows and pick up as for other wrinkles.

Row 20: Purl.
Row 21: K1, inc, k10, inc, k1. *(16 sts)*
Work 4 rows st st.
Row 26: To make a wrinkle, *pick up st from row 21, p2tog (st on needle and st picked up), p1, rep from * to end of row.***
Row 27: Cast (bind) off 8 sts, k to end (hold 8 sts on spare needle for Right Side of Body).

Left Front Leg

Work as for Right Front Leg to ***.
Row 27: K8, cast (bind) off 8 sts (leave 8 sts on spare needle for Left Side of Body).

Right Side of Body

Row 1: With to, cast on 1 st, with RS facing k8 from spare needle of Right Front Leg, cast on 6 sts. *(15 sts)*
Row 2: Purl.
Row 3: K15, cast on 6 sts. *(21 sts)*
Row 4: Purl.
Row 5: Inc, k20, cast on 8 sts, with RS facing k9 from spare needle of Right Back Leg. *(39 sts)*
Work 5 rows st st.
Row 11: Inc, k38. *(40 sts)*
Work 4 rows st st.
Row 16: P2tog, p37, inc. *(40 sts)*
Row 17: K14, cast (bind) off 12 sts, k to end. Work on last set of 14 sts.
Row 18: P14.
Row 19: Cast (bind) off 9 sts, k to end (hold 5 sts on spare needle for tail).
Row 20: With WS facing rejoin yarn to rem sts, p2tog, p12. *(13 sts)*
Row 21: K11, k2tog. *(12 sts)*
Row 22: P2tog, p10 (hold 11 sts on spare needle for right neck).

Left Side of Body

Row 1: With to, cast on 1 st, with WS facing p8 from spare needle of Left Front Leg, cast on 6 sts. *(15 sts)*
Row 2: Knit.

Row 3: P15, cast on 6 sts. *(21 sts)*
Row 4: Knit.
Row 5: Inc, p20, cast on 8 sts, with WS facing p9 from spare needle of Left Back Leg. *(39 sts)*
Work 5 rows st st.
Row 11: Inc, p38. *(40 sts)*
Work 4 rows st st.
Row 16: K2tog, k37, inc. *(40 sts)*
Row 17: P14, cast (bind) off 12 sts, p to end. Work on last set of 14 sts.
Row 18: K14.
Row 19: Cast (bind) off 9 sts, p to end (hold 5 sts on spare needle for tail).
Row 20: With RS facing rejoin yarn to rem sts, k2tog, k12. *(13 sts)*
Row 21: P11, p2tog. *(12 sts)*
Row 22: K2tog, k10 (hold 11 sts on spare needle for left neck).

Neck and Head

Row 1: With to and with RS facing, k11 held for neck from spare needle of Right Side of Body, then k11 held for neck from spare needle of Left Side of Body. *(22 sts)*
Row 2: Purl.
Work 5 rows st st.
Row 8: To make a wrinkle, *pick up st from row 2, p2tog (st on needle and st picked up), p1, rep from * to end of row.
Row 9: Knit.
Row 10: P1, p2tog, p16, p2tog, p1. *(20 sts)*
Row 11: Knit.
Row 12: P1, p2tog, p14, p2tog, p1. *(18 sts)*
Row 13: K15, wrap and turn (leave 3 sts on left-hand needle unworked).
Row 14: P12, w&t.
Row 15: Working top of head on centre 12 sts only, k12, w&t.
Row 16: P12, w&t.
Row 17: Knit across all sts. *(18 sts in total)*
Row 18: Purl.
Row 19: K14, w&t (leave 4 sts on left-hand needle unworked).

Legs

This elegant stance is achieved
with pipecleaners.

Head

For sewing up the head, refer to the diagrams on page 173.

Row 20: P10, w&t.
Row 21: Working top of head on centre 10 sts only, k10, w&t.
Row 22: P10, w&t.
Row 23: Knit across all sts. *(18 sts in total)*
Row 24: P2, [p2tog] 3 times, p2, [p2tog] 3 times, p2. *(12 sts)*
Work 5 rows st st.
Row 30: To make a wrinkle, *pick up st from row 24, [p2tog (st on needle and st picked up)] 4 times*, p4, rep from * to * once more.
Work 2 rows st st.
Join in mo.
Row 33: K2to, k8mo, k2to.
Row 34: P2to, p8mo, p2to.
Rep rows 33–34 once more.
Row 37: K3to, k6mo, k3to.
Row 38: P3to, p6mo, p3to.
Rep rows 37–38 twice more.
Row 43: K2togto, k2to, k4mo, k2to, k2togto. *(10 sts)*
Row 44: P2togto, p2to, p2mo, p2to, p2togto. *(8 sts)*
Cast (bind) off 8 sts.

Tail

Row 1: With to and with RS facing, k5 held for tail from spare needle of Left Side of Body, then k5 held for tail from spare needle of Right Side of Body. *(10 sts)*
Beg with a p row, work 3 rows st st.
Row 5: K2tog, k6, k2tog. *(8 sts)*
Work 3 rows st st.
Row 9: K2tog, k4, k2tog. *(6 sts)*
Work 7 rows st st.
Row 17: K2tog, k2, k2tog. *(4 sts)*
Work 3 rows st st.
Row 21: [K2tog] twice. *(2 sts)*
Row 22: P2tog and fasten off.

Tummy

With to, cast on 1 st.
Row 1: Inc. *(2 sts)*
Row 2: Purl.
Row 3: [Inc] twice. *(4 sts)*
Row 4: Purl.
Row 5: Inc, k2, inc. *(6 sts)*
Row 6: Purl.
Row 7: Inc, k4, inc. *(8 sts)*
Work 61 rows st st.
Row 69: K2tog, k4, k2tog. *(6 sts)*
Work 39 rows st st.
Cast (bind) off.

Ear

(make 2 the same)
With to, cast on 6 sts.
Work 4 rows st st.
Row 5: K2tog, k2, k2tog. *(4 sts)*
Row 6: Purl.
Row 7: [K2tog] twice. *(2 sts)*
Row 8: P2tog and fasten off.

Collar

With tx, cast on 30 sts.
Knit one row.
Cast (bind) off.

To Make Up

See also diagrams and notes on page 173.
SEWING IN ENDS Sew in ends, leaving ends from cast on and cast (bound) off rows for sewing up.
LEGS With WS together, fold leg in half. Starting at paw, sew up leg on RS.
BODY Sew along back of dog to tail.
TAIL Cut a pipecleaner 2.5cm (1in) longer than tail. Roll a little stuffing around pipecleaner, wrap tail around pipecleaner and sew up tail on RS, sewing down to just below root of tail. Protruding end of pipecleaner will vanish into body stuffing. Bend tail over back.

HEAD Fold cast (bound) off row of head in half and sew from nose to chin. Stuff head lightly. Thread tapestry needle with toffee yarn and fasten end to tip of nose. Take thread through head to emerge at top back (see diagrams on page 173), and pull up to form wrinkles. Fold nose in on itself to form jowls and sew centre of jowls to end of muzzle in middle of mo section (see photograph, right).

TUMMY Sew cast on row of tummy to where you have finished sewing down bottom, and sew cast (bound) off row to chin. Ease and sew tummy to fit body. Leave a 2.5cm (1in) gap between front and back legs on one side.

STUFFING Pipecleaners are used to stiffen the legs and help bend them into shape. Fold a pipecleaner into a 'U' shape and measure against front two legs. Cut to approximately fit, leaving an extra 2.5cm (1in) at both ends. Fold these ends over to stop pipecleaner poking out of paws. Roll a little stuffing around pipecleaner and slip into body, one end down each front leg. Repeat with second pipecleaner and back legs. Starting at the head, stuff the dog firmly, then sew up the gap. Sew up neck wrinkle across chest. Mould body into shape. If you want your dog to be more wrinkly, run a strand of toffee yarn from nose to bottom and back and pull up slightly for concertina effect.

EARS Sew cast on row of each ear to side of dog's head, following natural slope of head and with 5 sts between ears and with wrong side of ears facing downwards. Catch ears down with a stitch.

EYES With bl, sew 2 short horizontal satin stitches in front of large head wrinkle, as in photograph.

NOSE With bl, embroider nose in satin stitch.

COLLAR Sew ends of collar together and pop over head.

Lurcher

The ultimate lounge lizard, the Lurcher is elegant, graceful, beautiful, emotional and utterly faithful. A variable mix of a sight hound – Greyhound or Whippet – with another dog – typically a Bedlington Terrier or Border Collie – the Lurcher is the poacher's best friend. Traditionally a gypsy dog, the Lurcher has been adopted by families as the perfect pet. I know, I have one and she has won Prettiest Bitch three years in a row at the local dog show. She has now retired to bask in the glory of her victories.

Lurcher

Lurchers vary enormously; ours is a rough-coated whippet cross.

Measurements
Length: 15cm (6in)
Height to top of head: 14cm (5½in)

Materials
- Pair of 2¾mm (US 2) knitting needles
- Double-pointed 2¾mm (US 2) knitting needles (for holding stitches and for tail)
- 20g (¾oz) of Rowan Kidsilk Haze in Mud 652 (mu) used DOUBLE throughout
- 5g (⅙oz) of Rowan Kidsilk Haze in Smoke 605 (sm)
- NOTE: some parts of the dog use one strand of mu and one strand of sm held together, and this is called mus
- Small amount of Rowan Pure Wool 4ply in Eau de Nil 450 (en) for collar
- 2 pipecleaners for legs
- Tiny amount of Rowan Pure Wool 4ply in Black 404 (bl) for eyes and nose

Abbreviations
See page 172.
See page 172 for I-cord Technique.
See page 172 for Wrap and Turn Method.
See page 172 for Loopy Stitch. Work 2-finger loopy stitch throughout this pattern.

Right Back Leg
With mu, cast on 9 sts.
Beg with a k row, work 2 rows st st.
Row 3: Inc, k1, k2tog, k1, k2tog, k1, inc. *(9 sts)*
Row 4: Purl.
Row 5: K2tog, k5, k2tog.* *(7 sts)*
Work 5 rows st st.
Row 11: K2tog, inc, k1, inc, k2tog. *(7 sts)*
Row 12: Purl.
Row 13: K2tog, [inc] 3 times, k2tog. *(8 sts)*
Row 14: Purl.
Row 15: K2, [inc] 4 times, k2. *(12 sts)*
Row 16: Purl.
Row 17: K4, inc, k2, inc, k4. *(14 sts)*
Row 18: Purl.
Row 19: K5, inc, k2, inc, k5. *(16 sts)*
Row 20: Purl.
Row 21: K6, inc, k2, inc, k6. *(18 sts)*
Row 22: Purl.
Row 23: K7, inc, k2, inc, k7. *(20 sts)*
Work 3 rows st st.**
Row 27: Cast (bind) off 10 sts, k to end (hold 10 sts on spare needle for Right Side of Body).

Coat
For a flat-coated Lurcher, use Pure Wool 4ply yarn and don't work the loopy stitches.

Left Back Leg

Work as for Right Back Leg to **.
Row 27: K10, cast (bind) off 10 sts (hold 10 sts on spare needle for Left Side of Body).

Right Front Leg

Work as for Right Back Leg to *.
Work 9 rows st st.
Row 15: Inc, k5, inc. *(9 sts)*
Work 3 rows st st.
Row 19: Inc, k7, inc. *(11 sts)*
Row 20: Purl.***
Row 21: Cast (bind) off 5 sts, k to end (hold 6 sts on spare needle for Right Side of Body).

Left Front Leg

Work as for Right Front Leg to ***.
Row 21: K6, cast (bind) off 5 sts (hold 6 sts on spare needle for Left Side of Body).

Right Side of Body

Row 1: With mu, cast on 1 st, with RS facing k6 from spare needle of Right Front Leg, cast on 5 sts. *(12 sts)*
Row 2: Purl.
Row 3: Inc, k11, cast on 4 sts. *(17 sts)*
Row 4: Purl.
Row 5: K17, cast on 3 sts. *(20 sts)*
Row 6: Purl.
Row 7: Inc, k19, cast on 3 sts. *(24 sts)*
Row 8: Purl.
Row 9: K24, cast on 1 st, with RS facing k10 from spare needle of Right Back Leg, cast on 1 st. *(36 sts)*
Work 7 rows st st.
Row 17: K34, k2tog. *(35 sts)*
Row 18: P2tog, p33. *(34 sts)*
Row 19: K2tog, k30, k2tog. *(32 sts)*
Row 20: Cast (bind) off 22 sts, p to end (hold 10 sts on spare needle for right neck).

Left Side of Body

Row 1: With mu, cast on 1 st, with WS facing p6 from spare needle of Left Front Leg, cast on 5 sts. *(12 sts)*
Row 2: Knit.
Row 3: Inc, p11, cast on 4 sts. *(17 sts)*
Row 4: Knit.
Row 5: P17, cast on 3 sts. *(20 sts)*
Row 6: Knit.
Row 7: Inc, p19, cast on 3 sts. *(24 sts)*
Row 8: Knit.
Row 9: P24, cast on 1 st, with WS facing p10 from spare needle of Left Back Leg, cast on 1 st. *(36 sts)*
Work 7 rows st st.
Row 17: P34, p2tog. *(35 sts)*
Row 18: K2tog, k33. *(34 sts)*
Row 19: P2tog, p30, p2tog. *(32 sts)*
Row 20: Cast (bind) off 22 sts, p to end (hold 10 sts on spare needle for left neck).

Neck and Head

Row 1: With mu and with RS facing, k4, k2tog, k4 from spare needle of Right Side of Body, then k4, k2tog, k4 from spare needle of Left Side of Body. *(18 sts)*
Row 2: Purl.
Row 3: K4, k2tog, k6, k2tog, k4. *(16 sts)*
Row 4: Purl.
Row 5: K4, k2tog, k4, k2tog, k4. *(14 sts)*
Row 6: Purl.
Row 7: K11, wrap and turn (leave 3 sts on left-hand needle unworked).
Row 8: Working top of head on centre 8 sts only, p8, w&t.
Row 9: K8, w&t.
Rep rows 7–8 once more.
Row 12: P8, w&t.
Row 13: K1, loopy st 1, k1, loopy st 1, k1, loopy st 1, k1, loopy st 1, k3. *(14 sts in total)*
Row 14: Purl.
Join in sm and use mu/sn for loopy sts only, as given.

Row 15: K5mu, loopy st 1mus, k1mu, loopy st 1mus, k3mu, w&t (leave 3 sts on left-hand needle unworked).
Row 16: Working top of head on centre 8 sts only, p8mu, w&t.
Row 17: K1mu, loopy st 1mus, k1mu, loopy st 1mus, k1mu, loopy st 1mus, k2mu, w&t.
Row 18: P8mu, w&t.
Row 19: Loopy st 2mus, k4mu, loopy st 2mus, w&t.
Cont in mu.
Row 20: P8, w&t.
Row 21: K2, loopy st 1, k2, loopy st 1, k5. *(14 sts in total)*
Row 22: P2, p2tog, p2, p2tog, p2, p2tog, p2. *(11 sts)*
Work 2 rows st st.
Join in sm.
Row 25: K3mus, k5mu, k3mus.
Row 26: P4mus, p3mu, p4mus.
Row 27: K2togmus, k2mus, k3mu, k2mus, k2togmus. *(9 sts)*
Row 28: P3mus, p3mu, p3mus.
Row 29: K4mus, k1mu, k4mus.
Row 30: P2togmus, p5mus, p2togmus. *(7 sts)*
Cast (bind) off.

Tail

With two double-pointed needles and mu, cast on 6 sts.
Work i-cord as folls:
Knit 20 rows.
Row 21: K2tog, k2, k2tog. *(4 sts)*
Knit 6 rows.
Row 28: [K2tog] twice. *(2 sts)*
Row 29: K2tog and fasten off.

Tummy

With mu, cast on 5 sts.
Work 20 rows st st.
Row 21: K1, loopy st 1, k1, loopy st 1, k1.
Row 22: Purl.
Rep rows 21–22, 12 times more.
Work 38 rows st st.
Row 85: K2tog, k1, k2tog. *(3 sts)*
Work 3 rows st st.
Cast (bind) off.

Ear

(make 2 the same)
With mus, cast on 6 sts.
Knit 6 rows.
Row 7: K2tog, k2, k2tog. *(4 sts)*
Knit 2 rows.
Row 10: [K2tog] twice. *(2 sts)*
Row 11: K2tog and fasten off.

Collar

With en, cast on 24 sts.
Knit one row.
Cast (bind) off.

Body

Don't overstuff, this is a slim dog.

64

To Make Up

See also diagram and notes on page 173.

SEWING IN ENDS Sew in ends, leaving ends from cast on and cast (bound) off rows for sewing up.

LEGS With WS together, fold leg in half. Starting at paw, sew up leg on RS.

BODY Sew along back of dog and around bottom.

HEAD Fold cast (bound) off row of head in half and sew from nose to chin.

TUMMY Sew cast on row of tummy to bottom of dog's bottom (where back legs begin), and sew cast (bound) off row to chin. Ease and sew tummy to fit body. Leave a 2.5cm (1in) gap between front and back legs on one side.

STUFFING Pipecleaners are used to stiffen the legs and help bend them into shape. Fold a pipecleaner into a 'U' shape and measure against front two legs. Cut to approximately fit, leaving an extra 2.5cm (1in) at both ends. Fold these ends over to stop pipecleaner poking out of paws. Roll a little stuffing around pipecleaner and slip into body, one end down each front leg. Repeat with second pipecleaner and back legs. Starting at the head, stuff the dog firmly, then sew up the gap. Mould body into shape.

TAIL Sew cast on end of tail to dog where back meets bottom.

EARS Sew cast on row of each ear to side of dog's head, following natural slope of head and with 6 sts between ears.

EYES With bl, sew 2-loop French knots positioned as in photograph.

NOSE With bl, embroider nose in satin stitch.

COLLAR Sew ends of collar together and pop over head.

LOOPS Cut all loops and trim as desired.

Greyhound

Beautiful, gentle, affectionate and lazy, Greyhounds need far less exercise than you would imagine; a short burst of running then the rest of the day spent asleep on the sofa is their idea of heaven. Greyhounds are reputed to be one of the breeds that all other dogs are descended from. Greyhound owners are an eclectic bunch, ranging from Cleopatra, King Canute and Frederick the Great to Al Capone and Bart Simpson. Our Greyhound Jack Swan, RIP, was a lovely boy, missed by all.

Greyhound

A sleek dog, worked
in intarsia.

Measurements
Length: 20cm (8in)
Height to top of head: 16cm (6¼in)

Materials
- Pair of 2¾mm (US 2) knitting needles
- Double-pointed 2¾mm (US 2) knitting needles (for holding stitches and for tail)
- 20g (¾oz) of Rowan Cashsoft 4ply in Cream 433 (cr)
- 5g (⅙oz) of Rowan Cashsoft 4ply in Arran 456 (ar)
- Small amount of Rowan Pure Wool 4ply in Framboise 456 (fr) for collar
- 2 pipecleaners for legs
- Tiny amount of Rowan Pure Wool 4ply in Black 404 (bl) for eyes and nose
- 2 tiny black beads for eyes and sewing needle and black thread for sewing on

Abbreviations
See page 172.
See page 172 for Colour Knitting.
See page 172 for I-cord Technique.
See page 172 for Wrap and Turn Method.

Right Back Leg
With cr, cast on 6 sts.
Beg with a k row, work 2 rows st st.
Row 3: Inc, k1, k2tog, k1, inc. *(7 sts)*
Row 4 and every alt row: Purl.
Row 5: Inc, k5, inc. *(9 sts)*
Row 7: Inc, k1, k2tog, k1, k2tog, k1, inc. *(9 sts)*

Rep rows 7–8 twice more.
Work 2 rows st st.
Row 15: K2tog, k1, inc, k1, inc, k1, k2tog. *(9 sts)*
Row 16 and every alt row: Purl.
Row 17: Inc, k3, inc, k3, inc. *(12 sts)*
Row 19: Inc, k4, [inc] twice, k4, inc. *(16 sts)*
Row 21: Inc, k14, inc. *(18 sts)*
Row 23: Inc, k16, inc. *(20 sts)*
Row 25: Inc, k18, inc *(22 sts)*
Work 5 rows st st.
Row 31: Cast (bind) off 11 sts, k to end (hold 11 sts on spare needle for Right Side of Body).

Left Back Leg
With cr, cast on 6 sts.
Beg with a k row, work 2 rows st st.
Row 3: Inc, k1, k2tog, k1, inc. *(7 sts)*
Row 4 and every alt row: Purl.
Row 5: Inc, k5, inc. *(9 sts)*
Row 7: Inc, k1, k2tog, k1, k2tog, k1, inc. *(9 sts)*
Rep rows 7–8 twice more.
Work 2 rows st st.
Row 15: K2tog, k1, inc, k1, inc, k1, k2tog. *(9 sts)*
Row 16 and every alt row: Purl.
Row 17: Inc, k3, inc, k3, inc. *(12 sts)*
Join in ar.
Row 19: Incar, k2ar, k2cr, [inccr] twice, k4cr, inccr. *(16 sts)*
Row 20: P10cr, 6ar.
Row 21: Incar, k6ar, k8cr, inccr. *(18 sts)*
Row 22: P9cr, p9ar.
Row 23: Incar, k9ar, k7cr, inccr. *(20 sts)*
Row 24: P7cr, p13ar.
Row 25: Incar, k14ar, k4cr, inccr. *(22 sts)*
Row 26: P4cr, p18ar.
Cont in ar.
Work 4 rows st st.
Row 31: K11, cast (bind) off 11 sts (hold 11 sts on spare needle for Left Side of Body).

Shape
The legs are very slim: use a knitting needle to push the stuffing into the paws.

Legs

Pipecleaners are essential to help this dog stand up.

Right Front Leg

With cr, cast on 6 sts.
Beg with a k row, work 2 rows st st.
Row 3: Inc, [k2tog] twice, inc. *(6 sts)*
Row 4: Inc, p4, inc. *(8 sts)*
Row 5: Inc, k2tog, k2, k2tog, inc. *(8 sts)*
Row 6: Purl.
Row 7: Inc, k2tog, k2, k2tog, inc. *(8 sts)*
Row 8: Purl.
Row 9: Inc, k2, k2tog, k2, inc. *(9 sts)*
Row 10: Purl.
Join in ar.
Row 11: K6cr, k3ar.
Row 12: P4ar, p5cr.
Row 13: K4cr, k5ar.
Row 14: P5ar, p4cr.
Row 15: K3cr, k6ar.
Row 16: P6ar, p3cr.
Row 17: K3cr, k6ar.
Row 18: P6ar, p3cr.
Row 19: K4cr, k5ar.
Row 20: P4ar, p5cr.
Row 21: K6cr, k3cr.
Cont in cr.
Row 22: Purl.
Row 23: Inc, k7, inc. *(11 sts)*
Row 24: Purl.
Row 25: Inc, k9, inc. *(13 sts)*
Row 26: Purl.
Row 27: Cast (bind) off 6 sts, k to end (hold 7 sts on spare needle for Right Side of Body).

Left Front Leg

With cr, cast on 6 sts.
Beg with a k row, work 2 rows st st.
Row 3: Inc, [k2tog] twice, inc. *(6 sts)*
Row 4: Inc, p4, inc. *(8 sts)*
Row 5: Inc, k2tog, k2, k2tog, inc. *(8 sts)*
Row 6: Purl.
Row 7: Inc, k2tog, k2, k2tog, inc. *(8 sts)*
Row 8: Purl.
Row 9: Inc, k2, k2tog, k2, inc. *(9 sts)*
Work 13 rows st st.
Row 23: Inc, k7, inc. *(11 sts)*

Row 24: Purl.
Row 25: Inc, k9, inc. *(13 sts)*
Row 26: Purl.
Row 27: K7, cast (bind) off 6 sts (hold 7 sts on spare needle for Left Side of Body).

Right Side of Body

Row 1: With cr, cast on 1 st, with RS facing k7 from spare needle of Right Front Leg, cast on 3 sts. *(11 sts)*
Row 2: Purl.
Row 3: K11, cast on 4 sts. *(15 sts)*
Row 4: Purl.
Row 5: Inc, k14, cast on 3 sts. *(19 sts)*
Row 6: Purl.
Row 7: K19, cast on 4 sts. *(23 sts)*
Row 8: Purl.
Row 9: Inc, k22, cast on 3 sts. *(27 sts)*
Row 10: Purl.
Row 11: K27, with RS facing k11 from spare needle of Right Back Leg. *(38 sts)*
Join in ar.
Row 12: P3ar, p35cr.
Row 13: K32cr, k6ar.
Row 14: P9ar, p29cr.
Row 15: K26cr, k12ar.
Row 16: P12ar, p26cr.
Row 17: K27cr, k9ar, k2togar. *(37 sts)*
Row 18: P10ar, p27cr.
Row 19: Inccr, k26cr, k8ar, k2togar. *(37 sts)*
Row 20: Cast (bind) off 9 sts ar and 19 sts cr, p9cr icos (hold 9 sts on spare needle for right neck).

Left Side of Body

Row 1: With cr, cast on 1 st, with WS facing p7 from spare needle of Left Front Leg, cast on 3 sts. *(11 sts)*
Row 2: Knit.
Row 3: P11, cast on 4 sts. *(15 sts)*
Row 4: Knit.
Row 5: Inc, p14, cast on 3 sts. *(19 sts)*
Row 6: Knit.
Row 7: P19, cast on 4 sts. *(23 sts)*

Head

Manipulate the stuffing so that the head has an elegant curve.

Row 8: Knit.
Join in ar.
Row 9: Inccr, p4cr, p3ar, p15cr, cast on 3 sts cr. *(27 sts)*
Row 10: K16cr, k5ar, k6cr.
Row 11: P4cr, p9ar, p14cr, with WS facing p11ar from spare needle of Left Back Leg. *(38 sts)*
Row 12: K8ar, k15cr, k13ar, k2cr.
Row 13: P17ar, p13cr, p8ar.
Row 14: K8ar, k13cr, k17ar.
Row 15: P17ar, p15cr, p6ar.
Row 16: K5ar, k17cr, k16ar.
Row 17: P15ar, p19cr, p2ar, p2togar. *(37 sts)*
Row 18: K23cr, k14ar.
Row 19: Incar, k1ar, k23cr, k2togcr. *(37 sts)*
Row 20: Cast (bind) off 25 sts cr and 3 sts ar, k9ar icos (hold 9 sts on spare needle for left neck).

Neck and Head

Row 1: With cr and ar and with RS facing, k9cr from spare needle of Right Side of Body, then k9ar from spare needle of Left Side of Body. *(18 sts)*
Row 2: P1ar, p2togar, p6ar, p6cr, p2togcr, p1cr. *(16 sts)*
Row 3: K1cr, k2togcr, k10cr, k2togar, k1ar. *(14 sts)*
Cont in cr.
Row 4: Purl.
Row 5: K4, k2tog, k2, k2tog, k4. *(12 sts)*
Work 3 rows st st.
Row 9: Inc, k10, wrap and turn (leave 1 st on left-hand needle unworked).
Row 10: Working top of head on centre 10 sts only, p10, w&t.
Join in ar.
Row 11: K3ar, k7cr, w&t.
Row 12: P5cr, p5ar, w&t.
Row 13: K5ar, k5cr, w&t.
Row 14: P4cr, p6ar, w&t.
Row 15: K6ar, k4cr, inccr. *(14 sts in total)*
Row 16: P6cr, p6ar, p2cr.
Row 17: K3cr, k4ar, k7cr.
Row 18: P2togcr, p6cr, p2ar, p2cr, p2togcr. *(12 sts)*
Cont in cr.
Row 19: K10, w&t (leave 2 sts on left-hand needle unworked).
Row 20: Working top of head on centre 8 sts only, p8, w&t.
Row 21: K8, w&t.
Row 22: P8, w&t.
Row 23: K8, w&t.
Row 24: P8, w&t.
Row 25: Knit across all sts. *(12 sts in total)*
Row 26: P3, [p2tog] 3 times, p3. *(9 sts)*
Work 2 rows st st.
Row 29: K2tog, k5, k2tog. *(7 sts)*
Work 2 rows st st.
Row 32: P1, p2tog, p1, p2tog, p1. *(5 sts)*
Row 33: K2tog, k1, k2tog. *(3 sts)*
Cast (bind) off.

Tail

With two double-pointed knitting needles and cr, cast on 4 sts.
Work i-cord as folls:
Knit 5 rows.
Row 6: K2tog, k2. *(3 sts)*
Knit 10 rows.
Row 17: K2tog, k1. *(2 sts)*
Knit 6 rows.
Row 24: K2tog and fasten off.

Tummy

With cr, cast on 1 st.
Row 1: Inc. *(2 sts)*
Row 2: Purl.
Row 3: [Inc] twice. *(4 sts)*
Row 4: Purl.
Row 5: Inc, k2, inc. *(6 sts)*
Work 71 rows st st.
Row 77: K2tog, k2, k2tog. *(4 sts)*
Work 33 rows st st.
Row 111: [K2tog] twice. *(2 sts)*
Row 112: P2tog and fasten off.

Ear

(make 2 the same, 1 in ar and 1 in cr)
With cr, or with ar, cast on 5 sts.
Beg with a k row, work 4 rows st st.
Row 5: K2tog, k1, k2tog. *(3 sts)*
Row 6: Purl.
Row 7: K2tog, k1. *(2 sts)*
Row 8: P2tog and fasten off.

Collar

With fr, cast on 20 sts.
Row 1: Knit.
Row 2: Cast (bind) off 5 sts, k to end.
Row 3: K15.
Cast (bind) off.

To Make Up

See also diagram and notes on page 173.

SEWING IN ENDS Sew in ends, leaving ends from cast on and cast (bound) off rows for sewing up.

LEGS With WS together, fold leg in half. Starting at paw, sew up leg on RS.

BODY Sew along back of dog and and 2cm (¾in) down bottom.

TUMMY Sew cast on row of tummy to where you have finished sewing down bottom, and sew cast (bound) off row to chin. Ease and sew tummy to fit body. Leave a 2.5cm (1in) gap between front and back legs on one side.

STUFFING Pipecleaners are used to stiffen the legs and help bend them into shape. Fold a pipecleaner into a 'U' shape and measure against front two legs. Cut to approximately fit, leaving an extra 2.5cm (1in) at both ends. Fold these ends over to stop pipecleaner poking out of paws. Roll a little stuffing around pipecleaner and slip into body, one end down each front leg. Repeat with second pipecleaner and back legs. Starting at the head, stuff the dog firmly, then sew up the gap. Mould body into shape.

TAIL Sew cast on end of tail to dog where back meets bottom.

EARS Sew cast on row of each ear to side of dog's head, cream ear on cream side and brown ear on brown side, following natural slope of head and with 2 sts between ears.

EYES With bl, sew 2 short horizontal satin stitches positioned as in photograph. Sew beads to centre of each eye.

NOSE With bl, embroider nose in satin stitch.

COLLAR Sew ends of collar together and pop over head.

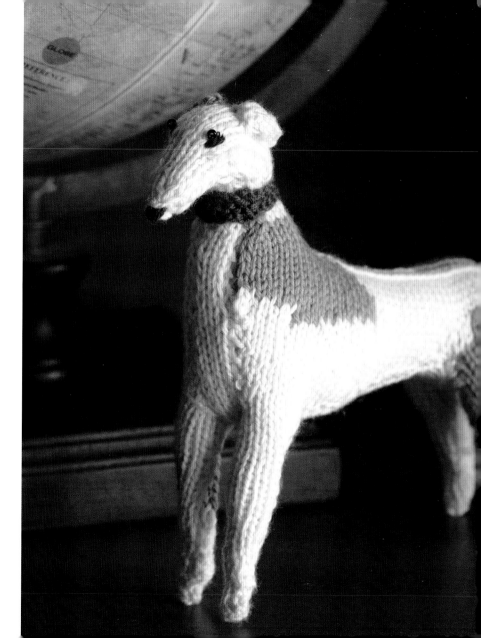

Terriers

Border Terrier

Small and rough-coated with otter-like heads, Border Terriers are immensely popular pets, being intelligent, friendly and companionable. They are working dogs and good at keeping vermin down, so best not kept with free-range hamsters or other small furry pets. Border Terriers played key roles in two films: *There's Something about Mary*, and Baxter was Ron Burgundy's beloved 'miniature Buddha, covered in hair' in *Anchorman*.

Border Terrier

Tweed yarn knits up to give the dog an authentic-looking variegated coat.

Measurements

Length: 14cm (5½in)
Height to top of head: 15cm (6in)

Materials

- Pair of 2¾mm (US 2) knitting needles
- Double-pointed 2¾mm (US 2) knitting needles (for holding stitches)
- 20g (¾oz) of Rowan Fine Tweed in Reeth 372 (re)
- 5g (⅙oz) of Rowan Kidsilk Haze in Wicked 599 (wk)
- NOTE: some parts of the dog use one strand of re and one strand of wk held together, and this is called rew
- Small amount of Rowan Cashsoft 4ply in Toxic 459 (tx) for collar
- 3 pipecleaners for legs and tail
- Tiny amount of Rowan Pure Wool 4ply in Black 404 (bl) for eyes and nose
- 2 tiny black beads for eyes and sewing needle and black thread for sewing on

Abbreviations

See page 172.
See page 172 for Wrap and Turn Method.
See page 172 for Loopy Stitch. Work 2-finger loopy stitch throughout this pattern.

Right Back Leg

With re, cast on 7 sts.
Beg with a k row, work 2 rows st st.
Row 3: Inc, k2tog, k1, k2tog, inc. *(7 sts)*
Row 4: Purl.
Rep rows 3–4 once more.
Work 6 rows st st.
Row 13: Inc, k5, inc. *(9 sts)*
Work 3 rows st st.
Row 17: K3, inc, k1, inc, k3. *(11 sts)*
Row 18: Purl.
Row 19: K4, inc, k1, inc, k4. *(13 sts)*
Row 20: Purl.*
Row 21: K5, inc, k1, inc, k5. *(15 sts)*
Row 22: Purl.
Row 23: K6, inc, k1, inc, k6. *(17 sts)*
Row 24: Purl.**
Row 25: Cast (bind) off 8 sts, k to end (hold 9 sts on spare needle for Right Side of Body).

Left Back Leg

Work as for Right Back Leg to **.
Row 25: K9, cast (bind) off 8 sts (hold 9 sts on spare needle for Left Side of Body).

Right Front Leg

Work as for Right Back Leg to *.
Row 21: Cast (bind) off 6 sts, k to end (hold 7 sts on spare needle for Right Side of Body).

Left Front Leg

Work as for Right Back Leg to *.
Row 21: K7, cast (bind) off 6 sts (hold 7 sts on spare needle for Left Side of Body).

Legs

Stuff the legs firmly so that the dog stands up straight.

Right Side of Body

Row 1: With re, cast on 1 st, with RS facing k7 from spare needle of Right Front Leg, cast on 3 sts. *(11 sts)*
Row 2: Purl.
Row 3: K11, cast on 3 sts. *(14 sts)*
Row 4: Purl.
Row 5: Inc, k13, cast on 3 sts. *(18 sts)*
Row 6: Purl.
Row 7: K18, with RS facing k9 from spare needle of Right Back Leg. *(27 sts)*
Work 4 rows st st.
Row 12: Inc, p26. *(28 sts)*
Join in wk.
Row 13: K8re, k10rew, k10re.
Row 14: P11re, p10rew, p7re.
Row 15: K7re, k12rew, k9re.
Row 16: P8re, p13rew, p7re.
Row 17: K7re, k14rew, k5re, k2togre. *(27 sts)*
Row 18: P2togre, p3re (hold 4 sts on spare needle for tail), cast (bind) off 14 sts rew, p8re icos (hold 8 sts on spare needle for right neck).

Left Side of Body

Row 1: With re, cast on 1 st, with WS facing p7 from spare needle of Left Front Leg, cast on 3 sts. *(11 sts)*
Row 2: Knit.
Row 3: P11, cast on 3 sts. *(14 sts)*
Row 4: Knit.
Row 5: Inc, p13, cast on 3 sts. *(18 sts)*
Row 6: Knit.
Row 7: P18, with WS facing p9 from spare needle of Left Back Leg. *(27 sts)*
Work 4 rows st st.
Row 12: Inc, k26. *(28 sts)*
Join in wk.
Row 13: P8re, p10rew, p10re.
Row 14: K11re, k10rew, k7re.
Row 15: P7re, p12rew, p9re.
Row 16: K8re, k13rew, k7re.
Row 17: P7re, p14rew, p5re, p2togre. *(27 sts)*
Row 18: K2togre, k3re (hold 4 sts on spare needle for tail), cast (bind) off 14 sts rew, k8re icos (hold 8 sts on spare needle for left neck).

Neck and Head

Row 1: With re and with RS facing, k8 from spare needle of Right Side of Body, then k8 from spare needle of Left Side of Body. *(16 sts)*
Row 2: Purl.
Row 3: K7, k2tog, k7. *(15 sts)*
Row 4: Purl.
Row 5: K1, inc, k11, inc, k1. *(17 sts)*
Row 6: Purl.

Head
The loopy stitch around the muzzle is cut quite short to give the characteristic bristly moustache.

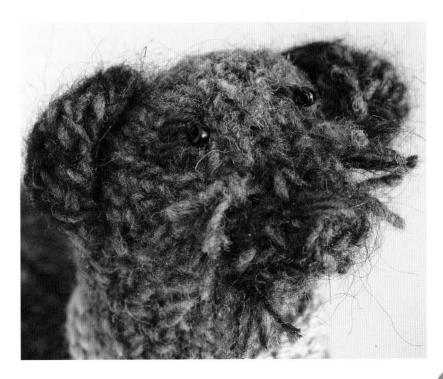

Row 7: K14, wrap and turn (leave 3 sts on left-hand needle unworked).
Row 8: Working top of head on centre 11 sts only, p11, w&t.
Row 9: K11, w&t.
Row 10: P11, w&t.
Row 11: K11, w&t.
Row 12: P11, w&t.
Row 13: Knit across all sts. *(17 sts in total)*
Row 14: Purl.
Row 15: K14, w&t (leave 3 sts on left-hand needle unworked).
Row 16: Working top of head on centre 11 sts only, p11, w&t.
Row 17: K11, w&t.
Row 18: P11, w&t.
Row 19: K11, w&t.
Row 20: P11, w&t.
Row 21: Knit across all sts. *(17 sts in total)*
Row 22: Purl.
Row 23: K2, [k2tog] twice, k5, [k2tog] twice, k2. *(13 sts)*
Row 24: P3, p2tog, p3, p2tog, p3. *(11 sts)*
Row 25: K2, k2tog, k3, k2tog, k2. *(9 sts)*
Row 26: Purl.
Join in wk and cont in rew.
Row 27: Loopy st 4, k1, loopy st 4.
Row 28: K2, k2tog, k1, k2tog, k2. *(7 sts)*
Row 29: Purl.
Cast (bind) off 7 sts.

Tail

Row 1: With re and with RS facing, k4 held for tail from spare needle of Left Side of Body, then k4 held for tail from spare needle of Right Side of Body. *(8 sts)*
Beg with a p row, work 3 rows st st.
Row 5: K2tog, k4, k2tog. *(6 sts)*
Work 8 rows st st.
Row 14: P2tog, p2, p2tog. *(4 sts)*
Work 2 rows st st.
Row 17: [K2tog] twice. *(2 sts)*
Row 18: P2tog and fasten off.

Tail

A pipecleaner is used to make an upright tail.

Tummy

With re, cast on 2 sts.
Row 1: [Inc] twice. *(4 sts)*
Row 2: Purl.
Row 3: Inc, k2, inc. *(6 sts)*
Row 4: Purl.
Row 5: Inc, k4, inc. *(8 sts)*
Work 39 rows st st.
Row 45: K2tog, k4, k2tog. *(6 sts)*
Work 13 rows st st.
Row 59: K2tog, k2, k2tog. *(4 sts)*
Work 13 rows st st.
Row 73: [K2tog] twice. *(2 sts)*
Row 74: Purl.
Row 75: K2tog and fasten off.

Ear

(make 2 the same)
With rew, cast on 7 sts.
Beg with a k row, work 2 rows st st.
Row 3: K2tog, k3, k2tog. *(5 sts)*
Row 4: Purl.
Row 5: K2tog, k1, k2tog. *(3 sts)*
Row 6: Purl.
Row 7: K2tog, k1. *(2 sts)*
Row 8: P2tog and fasten off.

Collar

With tx, cast on 26 sts.
Knit one row.
Cast (bind) off.

To Make Up

See also diagram and notes on page 173.

SEWING IN ENDS Sew in ends, leaving ends from cast on and cast (bound) off rows for sewing up.

LEGS With WS together, fold leg in half. Starting at paw, sew up leg on RS.

BODY Sew along back of dog to tail.

TAIL Cut a pipecleaner 2.5cm (1in) longer than tail. Roll a little stuffing around pipecleaner, wrap tail around pipecleaner and sew up tail on RS. Protruding end of pipecleaner will vanish into body stuffing.

HEAD Fold cast (bound) off row of head in half and sew from nose to chin.

TUMMY Sew cast on row of tummy to top of dog's bottom (just below tail), and sew cast (bound) off row to chin. Ease and sew tummy to fit body. Leave a 2.5cm (1in) gap between front and back legs on one side.

STUFFING Pipecleaners are used to stiffen the legs and help bend them into shape. Fold a pipecleaner into a 'U' shape and measure against front two legs. Cut to approximately fit, leaving an extra 2.5cm (1in) at both ends. Fold these ends over to stop pipecleaner poking out of paws. Roll a little stuffing around pipecleaner and slip into body, one end down each front leg. Repeat with second pipecleaner and back legs. Starting at the head, stuff the dog firmly, then sew up the gap. Mould body into shape.

EARS Sew cast on row of each ear to side of dog's head, with 5 sts between ears and with wrong side of ears facing downwards. Catch ears down with a stitch.

EYES With bl, sew 2 short horizontal satin stitches positioned as in photograph. Sew beads to centre of each eye.

MOUSTACHE Cut and trim loopy stitches to desired length.

NOSE With bl, embroider nose in satin stitch.

COLLAR Sew ends of collar together and pop over head.

Cairn Terrier

A big dog trapped in small dog's body, the Cairn originates from Scotland where it was bred for hunting vermin. Trapping its quarry down a hole, the dog would wait for its owner to come along and deal with the prey. Toto in *The Wizard Of Oz* was played by a Cairn called Terry; hard working, he appeared in a further thirteen films. Possibly inspired by her mother, Liza Minnelli owned several Cairns and the Duke and Duchess of Windsor owned two; the dog's food was specially prepared and spooned into silver bowls.

Cairn Terrier

The Cairn is a fairly complex dog to knit, with masses of cut loopy stitch.

Measurements

Length: 15cm (6in)
Height to top of head: 12cm (4¾in)

Materials

- Pair of 2¾mm (US 2) knitting needles
- Double-pointed 2¾mm (US 2) knitting needles (for holding stitches)
- 15g (½oz) of Rowan Kidsilk Haze in Mud 652 (mu)
- 10g (¼oz) of Rowan Kidsilk Haze in Ember 644 (em)
- NOTE: most of the dog uses one strand of mu and one strand of em held together, and this is called mue
- 5g (⅙oz) of Rowan Kidsilk Haze in Smoke 605 (sm)
- NOTE: the dog's muzzle uses one strand of mu and one strand of sm held together, and this is called mus
- Small amount of Rowan Cashsoft 4ply in Fennel 436 (fn) for collar
- 3 pipecleaners for legs and tail
- Tiny amount of Rowan Cashsoft 4ply in Black 422 (bl) for eyes and nose

Abbreviations

See page 172.
See page 172 for Wrap and Turn Method.
See page 172 for Loopy Stitch. Work 2-finger loopy stitch throughout this pattern.

Right Back Leg

With mue, cast on 11 sts.
Beg with a k row, work 2 rows st st.
Row 3: K3, k2tog, k1, k2tog, k3. (9 sts)
Row 4: Purl.
Row 5: K1, loopy st 1, k2tog, loopy st 1, k2tog, loopy st 1, k1. (7 sts)
Row 6: Purl.*
Row 7: K1, loopy st 1, k1, loopy st 1, k1, loopy st 1, k1.
Row 8: Purl.
Row 9: Inc, loopy st 1, k1, loopy st 1, k1, loopy st 1, inc. (9 sts)
Row 10: Purl.
Row 11: Inc, loopy st 1, k2, loopy st 1, k2, loopy st 1, inc. (11 sts)
Row 12: Purl.
Row 13: K1, loopy st 1, k2, inc, loopy st 1, inc, k2, loopy st 1, k1. (13 sts)
Row 14: Purl.
Row 15: K1, loopy st 1, k3, inc, loopy st 1, inc, k3, loopy st 1, k1. (15 sts)
Row 16: Purl.
Row 17: K1, loopy st 1, k4, inc, loopy st 1, inc, k4, loopy st 1, k1. (17 sts)
Row 18: Purl.**
Row 19: Cast (bind) off 8 sts, k to end (hold 9 sts on spare needle for Right Side of Body).

Left Back Leg

Work as for Right Back Leg to **.
Row 19: K9, cast (bind) off 8 sts (hold 9 sts on spare needle for Left Side of Body).

Right Front Leg

Work as for Right Back Leg to *.
Row 7: K1, loopy st 1, k2, loopy st 1, k2, loopy st 1, k1. (9 sts)
Row 8: Purl.
Rep rows 7–8 once more.
Row 11: Inc, loopy st 1, k2, loopy st 1, k2, loopy st 1, inc. (11 sts)
Row 12: Purl.***
Row 13: Cast (bind) off 5 sts, k to end (hold 6 sts on spare needle for Right Side of Body).

Coat

You can trim your Cairn's loops to be
as short or as long as you want.

Left Front Leg

Work as for Right Front Leg to ***.
Row 13: K6, cast (bind) off 5 sts (hold 6 sts
on spare needle for Left Side of Body).

Right Side of Body

Row 1: With mue, cast on 2 sts, with RS
facing k6 from spare needle of Right Front
Leg, cast on 4 sts. *(12 sts)*
Row 2: Purl.
Row 3: Inc, [loopy st 1, k1] 5 times, k1, cast
on 3 sts. *(16 sts)*
Row 4: Purl.
Row 5: Inc, k15, cast on 2 sts. *(19 sts)*
Row 6: Purl.
Row 7: K2, [loopy st 1, k1] 8 times, k1, with
RS facing [loopy st 1, k1] 4 times, k1 from
spare needle of Right Back Leg, cast on 2 sts.
(30 sts)
Work 3 rows st st.
Row 11: K1, [loopy st 1, k1] 14 times, k1.
Work 3 rows st st.
Row 15: K2, [loopy st 1, k1] 14 times.
Row 16: P2tog, p28. *(29 sts)*
Row 17: Knit.
Row 18: P2tog, p27. *(28 sts)*
Row 19: K1, [loopy st 1, k1] 12 times, k1,
k2tog. *(27 sts)*
Row 20: P6 (hold 6 sts on spare needle for
tail), cast (bind) off 11 sts, p to end (hold
10 sts on spare needle for right neck).

Left Side of Body

Row 1: With mue, cast on 2 sts, with WS
facing p6 from spare needle of Left Front
Leg, cast on 4 sts. *(12 sts)*
Row 2: Knit.
Row 3: Inc, p11, cast on 3 sts. *(16 sts)*
Row 4: K3, [loopy st 1, k1] 6 times, k1.
Row 5: Inc, p15, cast on 2 sts. *(19 sts)*
Row 6: Knit.
Row 7: P19, with WS facing p9 from spare
needle of Left Back Leg, cast on 2 sts. *(30 sts)*
Row 8: K2, [loopy st 1, k1] 14 times.
Work 3 rows st st.
Row 12: K1, [loopy st 1, k1] 14 times, k1.
Work 3 rows st st.
Row 16: K2, [loopy st 1, k1] 14 times.
Row 17: P28, p2tog. *(29 sts)*
Row 18: K2tog, [loopy st 1, k1] 13 times, k1.
(28 sts)
Row 19: P26, p2tog. *(27 sts)*
Row 20: K6 (hold 6 sts on spare needle for
tail) cast (bind) off 11 sts, k to end (hold
10 sts on spare needle for left neck).

Neck and Head

Row 1: With mue and with RS facing, k6,
k2tog, k2 held for neck from spare needle of
Right Side of Body, then k2, k2tog, k6 held
for neck from spare needle of Left Side of
Body. *(18 sts)*
Row 2: Purl.
Row 3: K2, loopy st 1, k1, loopy st 1, k2tog,
[loopy st 1, k1] 2 times, k2tog, loopy st 1, k1,
loopy st 1, k2. *(16 sts)*
Row 4: Purl.
Row 5: K13, wrap and turn (leave 3 sts on
left-hand needle unworked).
Row 6: Working top of head on centre 10 sts
only, p10, w&t.
Row 7: K1, [loopy st 1, k1] 4 times, k1, w&t.
Row 8: P10, w&t.
Row 9: K10, w&t.
Row 10: P10, w&t.

Head
Pinch the ears to make them stand up, giving the Cairn its pert look.

Row 11: K2, [loopy st 1, k1] 4 times, k3. *(16 sts in total)*
Row 12: Purl.
Row 13: K13, w&t (leave 3 sts on left-hand needle unworked).
Row 14: P10, w&t.
Row 15: [K1, loopy st 1] 5 times, w&t.
Row 16: P10, w&t.
Row 17: K10, w&t.
Row 18: P10, w&t.
Row 19: K3, loopy st 4, k6. *(16 sts)*
Row 20: P3, p2tog, p2, p2tog, p2, p2tog, p3. *(13 sts)*
Join in sm.
Row 21: K3mue, loopy st 3mus, k1mue, loopy st 3mus, k3mue. *(13 sts)*
Work 3 rows st st in mue.
Row 25: K1mue, loopy st 3mue, k2togmus, k1mus, k2togmus, loopy st 3mue, k1mue. *(11 sts)*
Cont in mus.
Row 26: Purl.
Row 27: K1, loopy st 2, k2tog, k1, k2tog, loopy st 2, k1. *(9 sts)*
Row 28: Purl.
Row 29: K1, loopy st 2, k3, loopy st 2, k1. Cast (bind) off.

Tail
Row 1: With mue and with RS facing, k4, k2tog held for tail from spare needle of Left Side of Body, then k2tog, k4 held for tail from spare needle of Right Side of Body. *(10 sts)*
Work 3 rows st st.
Row 5: K1, [loopy st 1, k1] 4 times, k1.
Row 6: Purl.
Row 7: K3, [k2tog] twice, k3. *(8 sts)*
Row 8: Purl.
Row 9: K1, loopy st 1, k4, loopy st 1, k1.
Row 10: Purl.
Row 11: K1, loopy st 1, [k2tog] twice, loopy st 1, k1. *(6 sts)*
Work 3 rows st st.

Row 15: [K2tog] 3 times. *(3 sts)*
Row 16: P3tog and fasten off.

Tummy
With mue, cast on 6 sts.
Beg with a k row, work 2 rows st st.
Row 3: K2tog, k2, k2tog. *(4 sts)*
Work 9 rows st st.
Row 13: Inc, k2, inc. *(6 sts)*
Work 23 rows st st.
Row 37: K2tog, k2, k2tog. *(4 sts)*
Work 5 rows st st.
Row 43: Inc, k2, inc. *(6 sts)*
Work 3 rows st st.
Row 47: K1, loopy st 1, k2, loopy st 1, k1.
Work 3 rows st st.
Rep last 4 rows 5 times more.
Work 4 rows st st.
Row 75: K2tog, k2, k2tog. *(4 sts)*
Work 3 rows st st.
Join in sm and cont in mus.
Row 79: K1, loopy st 2, k1.
Row 80: Purl.
Row 81: K1, loopy st 2, k1.
Row 82: [P2tog] twice. *(2 sts)*
Row 83: K2tog and fasten off.

Ear
(make 2 the same)
With mus, cast on 5 sts.
Knit 4 rows.
Row 5: K2tog, k1, k2tog. *(3 sts)*
Knit 2 rows.
Row 8: K3tog and fasten off.

Collar
With fn, cast on 24 sts.
Knit one row.
Cast (bind) off.

To Make Up

See also diagram and notes on page 173.

SEWING IN ENDS Sew in ends, leaving ends from cast on and cast (bound) off rows for sewing up.

LEGS With WS together, fold leg in half. Starting at paw, sew up leg on RS.

BODY Sew along back of dog to tail.

TAIL Cut a pipecleaner 2.5cm (1in) longer than tail. Roll a little stuffing around pipecleaner, wrap tail around pipecleaner and sew up tail on RS, sewing down to bottom of bottom (where back legs begin). Protruding end of pipecleaner will vanish into body stuffing.

HEAD Fold cast (bound) off row of head in half and sew from nose to chin.

TUMMY Sew cast on row of tummy to bottom of dog's bottom (where back legs begin), and sew cast (bound) off row to chin. Ease and sew tummy to fit body. Leave a 2.5cm (1in) gap between front and back legs on one side.

STUFFING Pipecleaners are used to stiffen the legs and help bend them into shape. Fold a pipecleaner into a 'U' shape and measure against front two legs. Cut to approximately fit, leaving an extra 2.5cm (1in) at both ends. Fold these ends over to stop pipecleaner poking out of paws. Roll a little stuffing around pipecleaner and slip into body, one end down each front leg. Repeat with second pipecleaner and back legs. Starting at the head, stuff the dog firmly, then sew up the gap. Mould body into shape.

EARS Sew cast on row of each ear to top of dog's head, just behind first row of mus loopy stitch, with 2 sts between ears.

EYES With bl, sew 3-loop French knots positioned as in photograph.

NOSE With bl, embroider nose in satin stitch.

COLLAR Sew ends of collar together and pop over head.

LOOPS Cut all loops and trim as desired.

Staffordshire Bull Terrier

Strong and courageous, the Staffie is descended from fighting dogs. Incorrectly thought to be an aggressive dog, they are – if trained properly – gentle, loyal and loving, and make ideal family pets. Half of the dogs in rehoming centres are Staffies or Staffie crossbreeds, so Battersea Dogs Home is trying to change the public's perception of this breed with a strong advertising campaign – 'Staffies are softer than you think' – featuring our own knitted version of a Staffie.

Staffordshire Bull Terrier

Our Staffie is sturdy and well-stuffed with a trademark studded collar.

Measurements

Length: 15cm (6in)
Height to top of head: 16cm (6¼in)

Materials

- Pair of 2¾mm (US 2) knitting needles
- Double-pointed 2¾mm (US 2) knitting needles (for holding stitches and for tail)
- 10g (¼oz) of Rowan Pure Wool 4ply in Snow 412 (sn)
- 15g (½oz) of Rowan Felted Tweed DK in Phantom 153 (ph)
- Small amount of Rowan Pure Wool 4ply in Black 404 (bl) for collar, eyes and nose
- 2 pipecleaners for legs
- 11 silver beads for collar and sewing needle and black thread for sewing on

Abbreviations

See page 172.
See page 172 for Colour Knitting.
See page 172 for I-cord Technique.
See page 172 for Wrap and Turn Method.

Right Back Leg

With sn, cast on 15 sts.
Beg with a k row, work 2 rows st st.
Row 3: Inc, k4, k2tog, k1, k2tog, k4, inc. *(15 sts)*
Row 4: Purl.
Rep rows 3–4 once more.*
Row 7: K5, k2tog, k1, k2tog, k5. *(13 sts)*
Row 8: P4, p2tog, p1, p2tog, p4.** *(11 sts)*
Work 2 rows st st.***
Join in ph.
Row 11: Incsn, k2sn, k2togsn, k1sn, k2togsn, k2sn, incsn. *(11 sts)*
Row 12: P3ph, p8sn.
Row 13: Incsn, k2sn, k2togsn, k1sn, k2togph, k2ph, incph. *(11 sts)*
Row 14: P6ph, p5sn.
Row 15: K4sn, incsn, k1ph, incph, k4ph. *(13 sts)*
Row 16: P8ph, p5sn.
Row 17: K5sn, incph, k1ph, incph, k2ph, incph, k2ph. *(16 sts)*
Row 18: P11ph, p5sn.
Row 19: K5sn, k1ph, incph, k1ph, incph, k3ph, incph, k3ph. *(19 sts)*
Row 20: P14ph, p5sn.
Row 21: K6sn, k1ph, incph, k1ph, incph, k9ph. *(21 sts)*
Row 22: P15ph, p6sn.
Row 23: K7sn, k1ph, incph, k1ph, incph, k10ph. *(23 sts)*
Row 24: P16ph, p7sn.
Row 25: Cast (bind) off 7 sts sn and 3 sts ph, k13ph icos (hold 13 sts on spare needle for Right Side of Body).

Left Back Leg

Work as for Right Back Leg to ***.
Join in ph.
Row 11: Incph, k2sn, k2togsn, k1sn, k2togsn, k2sn, incsn. *(11 sts)*
Row 12: P8sn, p3ph.
Row 13: Incph, k2ph, k2togph, k1sn, k2togsn, k2sn, incsn. *(11 sts)*
Row 14: P5sn, p6ph.
Row 15: K4ph, incph, k1ph, incsn, k4sn. *(13 sts)*
Row 16: P5sn, p8ph.
Row 17: K2ph, incph, k2ph, incph, k1ph, incph, k5sn. *(16 sts)*
Row 18: P5sn, p11ph.
Row 19: K3ph, incph, k3ph, incph, k1ph, incph, k1ph, k5sn. *(19 sts)*
Row 20: P5sn, p14ph.
Row 21: K9ph, incph, k1ph, incph, k1ph, k6sn. *(21 sts)*
Row 22: P6sn, p15ph.
Row 23: K10ph, incph, k1ph, incph, k1ph, k7sn. *(23 sts)*
Row 24: P7sn, p16ph.
Row 25: K13ph, cast (bind) off 3 sts ph and 7 sts sn (hold 13 sts on spare needle for Left Side of Body).

Right Front Leg

Work as for Right Back Leg to **.
Join in ph.
Row 9: K2togsn, k6sn, k1ph, k2togph. *(9 sts)*
Row 10: P5ph, p4sn.
Row 11: K2sn, k7ph.
Cont in ph.
Work 3 rows st st.
Row 15: Inc, k7, inc. *(11 sts)*
Row 16: Purl.
Row 17: K4, inc, k1, inc, k4. *(13 sts)*
Row 18: Purl.
Row 19: Inc, k11, inc. *(15 sts)*
Row 20: Purl.
Row 21: Cast (bind) off 7 sts, k to end (hold 8 sts on spare needle for Right Side of Body).

Left Front Leg

Work as for Right Back Leg to *.
Join in ph.
Row 7: K2ph, k3sn, k2togsn, k1sn, k2togsn, k5sn. *(13 sts)*
Row 8: P4sn, p2togsn, p1sn, p2togsn, p4ph. *(11 sts)*
Row 9: K2togph, k5ph, k2sn, k2togsn. *(9 sts)*
Cont in ph.
Work 5 rows st st.
Row 15: Inc, k7, inc. *(11 sts)*
Row 16: Purl.
Row 17: K4, inc, k1, inc, k4. *(13 sts)*
Row 18: Purl.
Row 19: Inc, k11, inc. *(15 sts)*
Row 20: Purl.
Row 21: K8, cast (bind) off 7 sts (hold 8 sts on spare needle for Left Side of Body).

Right Side of Body

Row 1: With ph, cast on 1 st, with RS facing k8 from spare needle of Right Front Leg, cast on 4 sts. *(13 sts)*
Row 2: Purl.
Row 3: K13, cast on 3 sts. *(16 sts)*
Row 4: Purl.
Row 5: Inc, k15, cast on 2 sts. *(19 sts)*
Row 6: Purl.
Join in sn.
Row 7: Incph, k18ph, cast on 2 sts sn, with RS facing k1sn, k12ph from spare needle of Right Back Leg, cast on 3 sts ph. *(38 sts)*
Row 8: P16ph, p2sn, p20ph.
Row 9: K21ph, k1sn, k16ph.
Work 4 rows st st in ph.
Row 14: P37ph, p1sn.
Row 15: K2sn, k36ph.
Row 16: P34ph, p4sn.
Row 17: K6sn, k28ph, k2togph, k2ph. *(37 sts)*
Row 18: P2ph, p2togph, p24ph, p9sn. *(36 sts)*
Row 19: K12sn, k20ph, k2togph, k2ph. *(35 sts)*

Row 20: Cast (bind) off 23 sts ph and 1 st sn, p11sn icos (hold 11 sts on spare needle for right neck).

Left Side of Body

Row 1: With ph, cast on 1 st, with WS facing p8 from spare needle of Left Front Leg, cast on 4 sts. *(13 sts)*
Row 2: Knit.
Row 3: P13, cast on 3 sts. *(16 sts)*
Row 4: Knit.
Row 5: Inc, p15, cast on 2 sts. *(19 sts)*
Row 6: Knit.
Join in sn.
Row 7: Incph, p18ph, cast on 2 sts sn, with WS facing p1sn, p12ph from spare needle of Left Back Leg, cast on 3 sts ph. *(38 sts)*
Row 8: K16ph, k2sn, k20ph.
Row 9: P21ph, p1sn, p16ph.
Work 4 rows st st in ph.
Row 14: K37ph, k1sn.
Row 15: P2sn, p36ph.
Row 16: K34ph, k4sn.
Row 17: P6sn, p28ph, p2togph, p2ph. *(37 sts)*
Row 18: K2ph, k2togph, k24ph, k9sn. *(36 sts)*
Row 19: P12sn, p20ph, p2togph, p2ph. *(35 sts)*
Row 20: Cast (bind) off 23 sts ph and 1 st sn, k11sn icos (hold 11 sts on spare needle for left neck).

Neck and Head

Row 1: With sn and with RS facing, k11 held for neck from spare needle of Right Side of Body, then k11 held for neck from spare needle of Left Side of Body. *(22 sts)*
Row 2: Purl.
Join in ph.
Row 3: K5sn, k2togsn, k1sn, k6ph, k1sn, k2togsn, k5sn. *(20 sts)*
Row 4: P5sn, p10ph, p5sn.
Row 5: K3sn, k2ph, k2togph, k6ph, k2togph, k2ph, k3sn. *(18 sts)*

Head

The ears are sewn on with the purl side on the outside, and will naturally curve inwards.

Body

The Staffie has an extremely wide chest.

Row 6: P2sn, p14ph, p2sn.
Cont in ph.
Row 7: K2, inc, k2, inc, k6, inc, k2, inc, k2. *(22 sts)*
Row 8: Inc, p20, inc. *(24 sts)*
Row 9: K18, wrap and turn (leave 6 sts on left-hand needle unworked).
Row 10: Working top of head on centre 12 sts only, p12, w&t.
Row 11: K12, w&t.
Rep rows 10–11 once more.
Row 14: P12, w&t.
Row 15: K18. *(24 sts in total)*
Join in sn.
Row 16: P11ph, p1sn, p12ph.
Row 17: K11ph, k2sn, k11ph.
Row 18: P11ph, p2sn, p11ph.
Row 19: K11ph, k2sn, k5ph, w&t (leave 6 sts on left-hand needle unworked).
Row 20: Working top of head on centre 12 sts only, p5ph, p2sn, p5ph, w&t.
Row 21: K4ph, k4sn, k4ph, w&t.
Row 22: P4ph, p4sn, p4ph, w&t.
Row 23: K4ph, k4sn, k4ph, w&t.
Row 24: P5ph, p2sn, p5ph, w&t.
Row 25: K5ph, k2sn, k11ph. *(24 sts in total)*
Row 26: P2ph, p2togph, p3ph, p2togph, p2ph, p2sn, p2ph, p2togph, p3ph, p2togph, p2ph. *(20 sts)*
Row 27: K2togph, k2ph, k2togph, k3ph, k1sn, k4ph, k2togph, k2ph, k2togph. *(16 sts)*
Cont in ph.
Row 28: P4, p2tog, p4, p2tog, p4. *(14 sts)*
Row 29: Knit.
Row 30: P3, p2tog, p4, p2tog, p3. *(12 sts)*
Row 31: Knit
Row 32: P2tog, p8, p2tog. *(10 sts)*
Row 33: Knit.
Cast (bind) off.

Tail

With two double-pointed knitting needles and ph, cast on 6 sts.
Work in i-cord as folls:
Knit 20 rows.
Row 21: K2tog, k2, k2tog. *(4 sts)*
Knit 4 rows.
Row 26: [K2tog] twice. *(2 sts)*
Row 27: K2tog and fasten off.

Tummy

With ph, cast on 6 sts.
Beg with a k row, work 4 rows st st.
Join in sn.
Row 5: K2ph, k2sn, k2ph.
Row 6: P1ph, p4sn, p1ph.
Row 7: K1ph, k4sn, k1ph.
Cont in sn.
Work 13 rows st st.
Row 21: Inc, k4, inc. *(8 sts)*
Work 19 rows st st.
Row 41: Inc, k6, inc. *(10 sts)*
Work 33 rows st st.
Row 75: K2tog, k6, k2tog. *(8 sts)*
Work 7 rows st st.
Row 83: K2tog, k4, k2tog. *(6 sts)*
Work 7 rows st st.
Row 91: K2tog, k2, k2tog. *(4 sts)*
Work 5 rows st st.
Cast (bind) off 4 sts.

Ear

(make 2 the same)
With ph, cast on 6 sts.
Beg with a k row, work 6 rows st st.
Row 7: K2tog, k2, k2tog. *(4 sts)*
Row 8: Purl.
Row 9: [K2tog] twice. *(2 sts)*
Row 10: P2tog and fasten off.

Collar

With bl, cast on 30 sts.
Knit 2 rows.
Cast (bind) off.

To Make Up

See also diagram and notes on page 173.

SEWING IN ENDS Sew in ends, leaving ends from cast on and cast (bound) off rows for sewing up.

LEGS With WS together, fold leg in half. Starting at paw, sew up leg on RS.

BODY Sew along back of dog and around bottom.

HEAD Fold cast (bound) off row of head in half and sew from nose to chin.

TUMMY Sew cast on row of tummy to bottom of dog's bottom (where back legs begin), and sew cast (bound) off row to chin. Ease and sew tummy to fit body. Leave a 2.5cm (1in) gap between front and back legs on one side.

STUFFING Pipecleaners are used to stiffen the legs and help bend them into shape. Fold a pipecleaner into a 'U' shape and measure against front two legs. Cut to approximately fit, leaving an extra 2.5cm (1in) at both ends. Fold these ends over to stop pipecleaner poking out of paws. Roll a little stuffing around pipecleaner and slip into body, one end down each front leg. Repeat with second pipecleaner and back legs. Starting at the head, stuff the dog firmly, then sew up the gap. Mould body into shape.

TAIL Sew cast on end of tail to dog where back meets bottom.

EARS Sew cast on row of each ear to side of dog's head, with wrong side of ears facing outwards. Attach at an angle sloping down towards back, so 6 sts between front of ears, 10 sts between back of ears. The ears will naturally curl around on themselves.

EYES With bl, sew 3-loop French knots positioned as in photograph.

NOSE With bl, embroider nose in satin stitch.

COLLAR Sew ends of collar together. Using black thread, sew beads to collar and pop over head.

Bedlington Terrier

While looking like a lamb, the Bedlington is reputed to have 'the heart of a lion'. They are friendly and entertaining, also opinionated, and like to be the centre of attention – as I think Dusty Jennings would agree. Rather oddly, although Lurchers are popular and Whippet Bedlington cross Lurchers are even more popular, Bedlingtons are fairly rare. The late Craigie Aitchison kept and painted beautiful Bedlingtons.

Bedlington Terrier

A lovely, shapely dog that
is easy to knit.

Measurements
Length: 17cm (6¾in)
Height to top of head: 14cm (5½in)

Materials
- Pair of 2¾mm (US 2) knitting needles
- Double-pointed 2¾mm (US 2) knitting needles (for holding stitches)
- 5g (⅛oz) of Rowan Cashsoft 4ply in Thunder 437 (th)
- 20g (¾oz) of Rowan Kidsilk Haze in Smoke 605 (sm)
- 10g (¼oz) of Rowan Kidsilk Haze in Ghost 642 (gh)
- NOTE: most of the dog uses two strands of sm and one strand of gh held together, and this is called smg
- Small amount of Rowan Pure Wool 4ply Raspberry 428 (ra) for collar
- 2 pipecleaners for legs
- 2 tiny black beads for eyes and sewing needle and black thread for sewing on
- Tiny amount of Rowan Pure Wool 4ply in Black 404 (bl) for nose

Abbreviations
See page 172.
See page 172 for Wrap and Turn Method.
NOTE: tail is worked during making up.

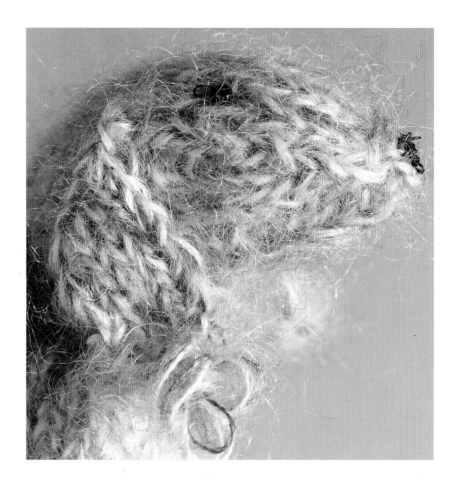

Head
The Bedlington has a sheep-like
convex head, and little loops
on the ends of its ears.

Right Back Leg

With th, cast on 7 sts.
Beg with a k row, work 2 rows st st.
Change to smg.
Row 3: Inc, k5, inc. (9 sts)
Row 4: Purl.
Row 5: Inc, k7, inc. (11 sts)
Work 5 rows st st.
Row 11: K2tog, k3, inc, k3, k2tog. (10 sts)
Row 12: Purl.
Row 13: K2tog, k1, [inc] 4 times, k1, k2tog.
(12 sts)
Row 14: Purl.
Row 15: K5, [inc] twice, k5. (14 sts)
Row 16: Purl.
Row 17: K6, [inc] twice, k6. (16 sts)
Row 18: Purl.
Row 19: K2tog, k4, [inc] 4 times, k4, k2tog.
(18 sts)
Row 20: Purl.
Row 21: K2tog, k5, [inc] 4 times, k5, k2tog.
(20 sts)
Work 3 rows st st.*
Row 25: Cast (bind) off 10 sts, k to end
(hold 10 sts on spare needle for Right Side
of Body).

Left Back Leg

Work as for Right Back Leg to *.
Row 25: K10, cast (bind) off 10 sts (hold
10 sts on spare needle for Left Side of Body).

Right Front Leg

With th, cast on 7 sts.
Beg with a k row, work 2 rows st st.
Change to smg.
Row 3: Inc, k5, inc. (9 sts)
Row 4: Purl.
Row 5: Inc, k7, inc. (11 sts)
Work 13 rows st st.**
Row 19: Cast (bind) off 5 sts, k to end (hold
6 sts on spare needle for Right Side of Body).

Left Front Leg

Work as for Right Front Leg to **.
Row 19: K6, cast (bind) off 5 sts (hold 6 sts
on spare needle).

Right Side of Body

Row 1: With smg and with RS facing, k6
from spare needle of Right Front Leg, cast
on 4 sts. (10 sts)
Row 2: Purl.
Row 3: K10, cast on 3 sts. (13 sts)
Row 4: Purl.
Row 5: K13, cast on 1 st. (14 sts)
Row 6: Purl.
Row 7: K14, cast on 1 st. (15 sts)
Row 8: Purl.
Row 9: K15, cast on 4 sts, with RS facing k10
from spare needle of Right Back Leg. (29 sts)
Row 10: P2tog, p27. (28 sts)
Row 11: Knit.
Row 12: P2tog, p25, inc. (28 sts)
Row 13: Knit.
Row 14: P2tog, p26. (27 sts)
Row 15: Knit.
Row 16: P2tog, p25. (26 sts)
Row 17: Knit.
Row 18: Cast (bind) off 3 sts, p to end. (23 sts)
Row 19: K7, k2tog, cast (bind) off 14 sts
(hold 8 sts on spare needle for right neck).

Left Side of Body

Row 1: With smg and with WS facing, p6
from spare needle of Left Front Leg, cast on
4 sts. (10 sts)
Row 2: Knit.
Row 3: P10, cast on 3 sts. (13 sts)
Row 4: Knit.
Row 5: P13, cast on 1 st. (14 sts)
Row 6: Knit.
Row 7: P14, cast on 1 st. (15 sts)
Row 8: Knit.
Row 9: P15, cast on 4 sts, with WS facing
p10 from spare needle of Left Back Leg.
Row10: K2tog, k27. (28 sts)

Row 11: Purl.
Row 12: K2tog, k25, inc. *(28 sts)*
Row 13: Purl.
Row 14: K2tog, k26. *(27 sts)*
Row 15: Purl.
Row 16: K2tog, k25. *(26 sts)*
Row 17: Purl.
Row 18: Cast (bind) off 3 sts, k to end. *(23 sts)*
Row 19: P7, p2tog, cast (bind) off 14 sts (hold 8 sts for on spare needle for left neck).

Tail

The Bedlington's skinny little tail is made with buttonhole stitch (see page 173).

Neck and Head

Row 1: With smg and with RS facing, k8 held for neck from spare needle of Right Side of Body, then k8 held for neck from spare needle of Left Side of Body. *(16 sts)*
Row 2: P7, p2tog, p7. *(15 sts)*
Row 3: Knit.
Row 4: P5, p2tog, p1, p2tog, p5. *(13 sts)*
Row 5: K10, wrap and turn (leave 3 sts on left-hand needle unworked).
Row 6: Working top of head on centre 7 sts only, p7, w&t.
Row 7: K7, w&t.
Row 8: P7, w&t.
Row 9: K7, w&t.
Row 10: P7, w&t.
Row 11: K7, w&t.
Row 12: P7, w&t.
Row 13: Knit across all sts. *(13 sts in total)*
Row 14: Purl.
Row 15: K2tog, k9, k2tog. *(11 sts)*
Row 16: Purl.
Row 17: Knit.
Row 18: P2, p2tog, p3, p2tog, p2. *(9 sts)*
Row 19: Knit.
Row 20: P1, p2tog, p3, p2tog, p1. *(7 sts)*
Row 21: K2tog, k3, k2tog. *(5 sts)*
Cast (bind) off.

Tummy

With smg, cast on 3 sts.
Row 1: Knit.
Row 2: Purl.

Row 3: Inc, k1, inc. *(5 sts)*
Row 4: Purl.
Row 5: Inc, k3, inc. *(7 sts)*
Work 45 rows st st.
Row 51: K2tog, k3, k2tog. *(5 sts)*
Work 13 rows st st.
Row 65: K2tog, k1, k2tog. *(3 sts)*
Row 66: Purl.
Cast (bind) off.

Right Ear

With smg, cast on 2 sts.
Beg with a k row, work 2 rows st st.
Row 3: [Inc] twice. *(4 sts)*
Row 4: Purl.
Row 5: Inc, k2, inc. *(6 sts)*
Row 6: Purl.
Work 4 rows st st.***
Row 11: K4, k2tog. *(5 sts)*
Row 12: P2tog, p3. *(4 sts)*
Row 13: K2, k2tog. *(3 sts)*
Cast (bind) off.

Left Ear

Work as for Right Ear to ***.
Row 11: K2tog, k4. *(5 sts)*
Row 12: P3, p2tog. *(4 sts)*
Row 13: K2tog, k2. *(3 sts)*
Cast (bind) off.

Collar

With ra, cast on 26 sts.
Knit one row.
Cast (bind) off.

To Make Up

See also diagrams and notes on page 173.
SEWING IN ENDS Sew in ends, leaving ends from cast on and cast (bound) off rows for sewing up.
LEGS With WS together, fold leg in half. Starting at paw, sew up leg on RS.
BODY Sew along back of dog and around bottom.

TUMMY Sew cast on row of tummy to top of dog's bottom (where it meets end of back), and sew cast (bound) off row to chin. Ease and sew tummy to fit body. Leave a 2.5cm (1in) gap between front and back legs on one side.

STUFFING Pipecleaners are used to stiffen the legs and help bend them into shape. Fold a pipecleaner into a 'U' shape and measure against front two legs. Cut to approximately fit, leaving an extra 2.5cm (1in) at both ends. Fold these ends over to stop pipecleaner poking out of paws. Roll a little stuffing around pipecleaner and slip into body, one end down each front leg. Repeat with second pipecleaner and back legs. Starting at the head, stuff the dog firmly, then sew up the gap. Mould body into shape.

TAIL With smg make a 7cm (2¾in) loop where back meets bottom (see diagrams on page 173). Using same yarn and starting at the end near bottom, cover loop with tightly packed buttonhole stitch. When complete, thread yarn up through tail and trim.

EARS Sew cast on row of each ear to side of dog's head, right ear on right side and left ear on left side, with 2 sts between ears and with wrong side of ears facing downwards. Thread tapestry needle with smg and embroider three 5mm (¼in) loops on end of each ear. Catch ears down with a stitch.

EYES Sew on black beads, positioned as in photograph.

NOSE With bl, embroider nose in satin stitch.

COLLAR Sew ends of collar together and pop over head.

Yorkshire Terrier

Tiny but feisty, the Yorkshire Terrier was originally bred to catch rats in Victorian clothing mills in Yorkshire. Huddersfield Ben was, reportedly, the best stud of his breed and most current show Yorkies are his descendants. The smallest dog ever recorded was a Yorkshire Terrier called Sylvia, from Blackburn, who measured a mere 2½ inches high and 3½ inches long and weighed just 4 ounces. Hugely popular in Hollywood, celebrities photographed clutching their Yorkies include Audrey Hepburn, Britney Spears, Orlando Bloom, Venus Williams and Justin Timberlake.

Yorkshire Terrier

The Yorkie is knitted in double mohair to make the most of the fluffy and soft coat.

Measurements

Length: 15cm (6in)
Height to top of head: 13cm (5in)

Materials

- Pair of 2¾mm (US 2) knitting needles
- Double-pointed 2¾mm (US 2) knitting needles (for holding stitches and for tail)
- 15g (½oz) of Rowan Kidsilk Haze in Ember 644 (em) used DOUBLE throughout
- 15g (½oz) of Rowan Kidsilk Haze in Wicked 599 (wk) used DOUBLE throughout
- 2 pipecleaners for legs
- Tiny amount of Rowan Pure Wool 4ply in Black 404 (bl) for eyes and nose
- Small amount of Rowan Pure Wool 4ply in Raspberry 428 (ra) for bow

Abbreviations

See page 172.
See page 172 for Colour Knitting.
See page 172 for I-cord Technique.
See page 172 for Wrap and Turn Method.
See page 172 for Loopy Stitch. Work 3-finger loopy stitch throughout this pattern.

Right Back Leg

With em, cast on 9 sts.
Beg with a k row, work 2 rows st st.
Row 3: K2, k2tog, k1, k2tog, k2. *(7 sts)*
Work 3 rows st st.*
Row 7: Inc, loopy st 1, k3, loopy st 1, inc. *(9 sts)*
Row 8: Purl.
Row 9: Inc, loopy st 1, k2, loopy st 1, k2, loopy st 1, inc. *(11 sts)*
Row 10: Purl.
Row 11: K1, loopy st 1, k2, inc, loopy st 1, inc, k2, loopy st 1, k1. *(13 sts)*
Row 12: Purl.
Row 13: K1, loopy st 1, k3, inc, loopy st 1, inc, k3, loopy st 1, k1. *(15 sts)*
Row 14: Purl.**
Row 15: Cast (bind) off 7 sts, k to end (hold 8 sts on spare needle for Right Side of Body).

Left Back Leg

Work as for Right Back Leg to **.
Row 15: K8, cast (bind) off 7 sts (hold 8 sts on spare needle for Left Side of Body).

Right Front Leg

Work as for Right Back Leg to *.
Row 7: K1, loopy st 1, k3, loopy st 1, k1.
Row 8: Purl.
Row 9: Inc, loopy st 1, k1, loopy st 1, k1, loopy st 1, inc. *(9 sts)*
Row 10: Purl.
Row 11: K1, loopy st 1, k2, loopy st 1, k2, loopy st 1, k1.
Row 12: Purl.***
Row 13: Cast (bind) off 4 sts, k to end (hold 5 sts on spare needle for Right Side of Body).

Left Front Leg

Work as for Right Front Leg to ***.
Row 13: K5, cast (bind) off 4 sts (hold 5 sts on spare needle for Left Side of Body).

Tables

Tail

The tail doesn't need a pipecleaner to make it perky.

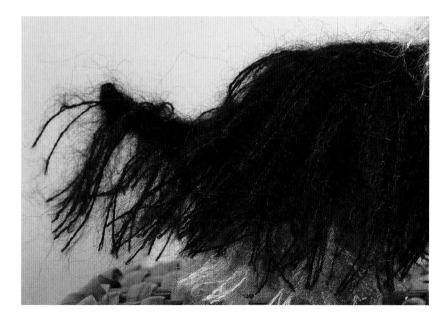

Right Side of Body

Row 1: With em and wk, cast on 1 st em, with RS facing k3em, k2wk from spare needle of Right Front Leg, cast on 3 sts wk. *(9 sts)*

Row 2: P6wk, p3em.

Row 3: Incem, loopy st 1em, k1em, [loopy st 1wk, k1wk] 3 times, cast on 2 sts wk. *(12 sts)*

Row 4: P9wk, p3em.

Row 5: Incem, k1em, k10wk, cast on 2 sts wk, k8wk from spare needle of Right Back Leg, cast on 2 sts wk. *(25 sts)*

Row 6: P23wk, p2em.

Row 7: K1em, loopy st 1em, [k1wk, loopy st 1wk] 11 times, k1wk.

Row 8: P24wk, p1em.

Cont in wk.

Row 9: Knit.

Row 10: Purl.

Row 11: [K1, loopy st 1] 12 times, k1. Work 3 rows st st.

Row 15: [K1, loopy st 1] 12 times, k1.

Row 16: P2tog, p23. *(24 sts)*

Row 17: [K1, loopy st 1] 11 times, k2tog. *(23 sts)*

Row 18: Cast (bind) off 14 sts, p to end (hold 9 sts on spare needle for right neck).

Left Side of Body

Row 1: With em and wk, cast on 1 st em, with WS facing p3em, p2wk from spare needle of Left Front Leg, cast on 3 sts wk. *(9 sts)*

Row 2: [K1wk, loopy st 1wk] 3 times, k1em, loopy st 1em, k1em.

Row 3: Incem, p2em, p6wk, cast on 2 sts wk. *(12 sts)*

Row 4: K9wk, k3em.

Row 5: Incem, p1em, p10wk, cast on 2 sts wk, p8wk from spare needle of Left Back Leg, cast on 2 sts wk. *(25 sts)*

Row 6: [K1wk, loopy st 1wk] 11 times, k1wk, k2em.

Row 7: P2em, p23wk.

Row 8: K24wk, k1em.

Cont in wk.

Row 9: Purl.

Row 10: [K1, loopy st 1] 12 times, k1. Work 3 rows st st.

Row 14: [K1, loopy st 1] 12 times, k1.

Row 15: Purl.

Row 16: K2tog, [loopy st 1, k1] 11 times, k1. *(24 sts)*

Row 17: P22, p2tog. *(23 sts)*

Row 18: Cast (bind) off 14 sts, k to end (hold 9 sts on spare needle for left neck).

Neck and Head

Row 1: With em and wk and with RS facing, k2em, k7wk from spare needle of Right Side of Body, then k7wk, k2em from spare needle of Left Side of Body. *(18 sts)*

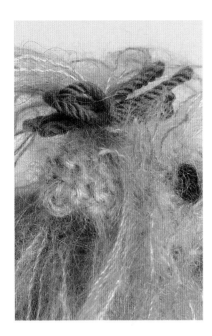

Head

Use a tiny amount of pink (or whatever colour you want) wool to tie up the topknot.

Row 2: P5em, p8wk, p5em.
Row 3: [K1em, loopy st 1em] 3 times, k1em, [loopy st 1wk, k1wk] 2 times, [loopy st 1em, k1em] 3 times, loopy st 1em.
Cont in em.
Row 4: Purl.
Row 5: K4, k2tog, k6, k2tog, k4. *(16 sts)*
Row 6: Purl.
Row 7: [K1, loopy st 1] 6 times, k1, wrap and turn (leave 3 sts on left-hand needle unworked).
Row 8: Working top of head on centre 10 sts only, p10, w&t.
Row 9: [K1, loopy st 1] 5 times, w&t.
Row 10: P10, w&t.
Row 11: [Loopy st 1, k1] 5 times, w&t.
Row 12: P10, w&t.
Row 13: [K1, loopy st 1] 6 times, k1. *(16 sts in total)*
Row 14: Purl.
Row 15: [K1, loopy st 1] 6 times, w&t (leave 4 sts on left-hand needle unworked).
Row 16: Working top of head on centre 8 sts only, p8, w&t.
Row 17: [Loopy st 1, k1] 4 times, w&t.
Row 18: P8, w&t.
Row 19: [K1, loopy st 1] 4 times, w&t.
Row 20: P8, w&t.
Row 21: [Loopy st 1, k1] 6 times. *(16 sts in total)*
Row 22: P3, p2tog, p2, p2tog, p2, p2tog, p3. *(13 sts)*
Row 23: K2, loopy st 4, k1, loopy st 4, k2.
Row 24: Purl.
Row 25: K1, loopy st 2, k2tog, k3, k2tog, loopy st 2, k1. *(11 sts)*
Row 26: Purl.
Row 27: K1, loopy st 2, k5, loopy st 2, k1.
Row 28: Purl.
Row 29: K1, loopy st 2, k2tog, k1, k2tog, loopy st 2, k1. *(9 sts)*
Row 30: P2tog, p5, p2tog. *(7 sts)*
Cast (bind) off.

Tail

With two double-pointed knitting needles and wk, cast on 6 sts.
Work in i-cord as folls:
Knit 2 rows.
Row 3: K1, loopy st 1, k2, loopy st 1, k1.
Rep last 3 rows 3 times more.
Row 13: Knit.
Row 14: K2tog, k2, k2tog. *(4 sts)*
Row 15: K1, loopy st 2, k1.
Work 2 rows st st.
Row 18: K1, loopy st 2, k1.
Row 19: [K2tog] twice. *(2 sts)*
Row 20: K2tog and fasten off.

Tummy

With em, cast on 6 sts.
Beg with a k row, work 2 rows st st.
Row 3: K2tog, k2, k2tog. *(4 sts)*
Work 9 rows st st.
Row 13: Inc, k2, inc. *(6 sts)*
Work 19 rows st st.
Row 33: K2tog, k2, k2tog. *(4 sts)*
Work 3 rows st st.
Row 37: Inc, k2, inc. *(6 sts)*
Work 3 rows st st.
Row 41: K1, loopy st 1, k2, loopy st 1, k1.
Work 3 rows st st.
Rep last 4 rows 4 times more.
Work 2 rows st st.
Row 63: K2tog, k2, k2tog. *(4 sts)*
Work 8 rows st st.
Row 72: [P2tog] twice. *(2 sts)*
Row 73: K2tog and fasten off.

Ear

(make 2 the same)
With em, cast on 5 sts.
Knit 4 rows.
Row 5: K2tog, k1, k2tog. *(3 sts)*
Knit 2 rows.
Row 8: K3tog and fasten off.

To Make Up

See also diagram and notes on page 173.

SEWING IN ENDS Sew in ends, leaving ends from cast on and cast (bound) off rows for sewing up.

LEGS With WS together, fold leg in half. Starting at paw, sew up leg on RS.

BODY Sew along back of dog and around bottom.

HEAD Fold cast (bound) off row of head in half and sew from nose to chin.

TUMMY Sew cast on row of tummy to bottom of dog's bottom (where back legs begin), and sew cast (bound) off row to chin, matching curves of tummy to legs. Ease and sew tummy to fit body. Leave a 2.5cm (1in) gap between front and back legs on one side.

STUFFING Pipecleaners are used to stiffen the legs and help bend them into shape. Fold a pipecleaner into a 'U' shape and measure against front two legs. Cut to approximately fit, leaving an extra 2.5cm (1in) at both ends. Fold these ends over to stop pipecleaner poking out of paws. Roll a little stuffing around pipecleaner and slip into body, one end down each front leg. Repeat with second pipecleaner and back legs. Starting at the head, stuff the dog firmly, then sew up the gap. Mould body into shape.

TAIL Sew cast on end of tail to dog where back meets bottom.

EARS Sew cast on row of each ear to top of dog's head, just behind second row of loopy stitch, with 3 sts between ears.

EYES With bl, sew 3-loop French knots positioned as in photograph.

NOSE With bl, embroider nose in satin stitch.

LOOPS Cut all loops and trim as desired.

TOPKNOT Scoop up about 8 tufts from on top of head and secure with 2 lengths of ra tied in a bow.

Airedale Terrier

'**King of Terriers**', Airedales are the largest of the terrier family and were originally named after the Aire Valley in West Yorkshire. The Airedale is multi-talented: it can be used for hunting, as a watchdog, and in police and military work. The Airedale could also be described as 'war dog', because over 3,000 Airedales were recruited for military service in WWI. They were used for locating wounded soldiers and carrying messages behind enemy lines. Sadly, two Airedales went down on the *Titanic*.

Airedale Terrier

This Airedale is knitted in tweed to give the characteristic rough-coated look.

Measurements

Length: 16cm (6¼in)
Height to top of head: 17cm (6¾in)

Materials

- Pair of 2¾mm (US 2) knitting needles
- Double-pointed 2¾mm (US 2) knitting needles (for holding stitches)
- 20g (¾oz) of Rowan Fine Tweed in Reeth 372 (re)
- 10g (¼oz) of Rowan Fine Tweed in Pendle 377 (pd)
- Small amount of Rowan Cashsoft 4ply in Fennel 436 (fn) for collar
- 3 pipecleaners for legs and tail
- Tiny amount of Rowan Cashsoft 4ply in Black 422 (bl) for eyes and nose

Abbreviations

See page 172.
See page 172 for Colour Knitting.
See page 172 for Wrap and Turn Method.
See page 172 for Loopy Stitch. Work 2-finger loopy stitch throughout this pattern.

Right Back Leg

With re, cast on 11 sts.
Beg with a k row, work 2 rows st st.
Row 3: Inc, k2, k2tog, k1, k2tog, k2, inc. *(11 sts)*
Row 4: Purl.
Rep rows 3–4 once more.
Row 7: K2tog, k7, k2tog.* *(9 sts)*
Work 3 rows st st.
Row 11: K2tog, k1, inc, k1, inc, k1, k2tog. *(9 sts)*
Row 12: Purl.
Rep rows 11–12 once more.
Work 4 rows st st.
Row 19: K3, inc, k1, inc, k3. *(11 sts)*
Row 20: Purl.
Row 21: K4, inc, k1, inc, k4. *(13 sts)*
Row 22: Purl.
Row 23: K5, inc, k1, inc, k5. *(15 sts)*
Row 24: Purl.
Row 25: K6, inc, k1, inc, k6. *(17 sts)*
Row 26: Purl.**
Row 27: Cast (bind) off 8 sts, k to end (hold 9 sts on spare needle for Right Side of Body).

Left Back Leg

Work as for Right Back Leg to **.
Row 27: K9, cast (bind) off 8 sts (hold 9 sts on spare needle for Left Side of Body).

Right Front Leg

Work as for Right Back Leg to *.
Work 7 rows st st.
Row 15: Inc, k7, inc. *(11 sts)*
Work 3 rows st st.
Row 19: Inc, k9, inc. *(13 sts)*
Row 20: Purl.***
Row 21: Cast (bind) off 6 sts, k to end (hold 7 sts on spare needle for Right Side of Body).

Left Front Leg

Work as for Right Front Leg to ***.
Row 21: K7, cast (bind) off 6 sts (hold 7 sts on spare needle for Left Side of Body).

Right Side of Body

Row 1: With re, cast on 1 st, with RS facing k7 from spare needle of Right Front Leg, cast on 6 sts. *(14 sts)*
Row 2: Purl.
Join in pd.
Row 3: Incre, k9re, k4pd, cast on 4 sts pd. *(19 sts)*
Row 4: P8pd, p11re.
Row 5: K10re, k9pd, cast on 4 sts pd. *(23 sts)*
Row 6: P13pd, p10re.
Row 7: K10re, k13pd, cast on 2 sts pd and 1 st re, with RS facing k9re from spare needle of Right Back Leg, cast on 2 sts re. *(37 sts)*
Row 8: P12re, p15pd, p10re.
Row 9: K10re, k15pd, k12re.
Row 10: P11re, p16pd, p10re.
Row 11: K10re, k16pd, k11re.
Row 12: P11re, p16pd, p10re.
Row 13: K10re, k17pd, k10re.
Row 14: P10re, p17pd, p10re.
Row 15: K11re, k17pd, k9re.
Row 16: P8re, p18pd, p6re, p2pd, p3re.
Row 17: K4re, k2pd, k5re, k18pd, k8re.
Row 18: P6re, p20pd, p4re, p1pd, p3re, p2pd, p1re.
Row 19: K1re, k3pd, k6re, k23pd, k2re, k2togre. *(36 sts)*
Row 20: P2togre, p26pd, p3re, p2pd, p3re. *(35 sts)*
Row 21: K4re, k7pd (hold 11 sts on spare needle for right neck), cast (bind) off 19 sts pd, k3pd icos, k2re (hold 5 sts on spare needle for tail).

Left Side of Body

Row 1: With re, cast on 1 st, with WS facing p7 from spare needle of Left Front Leg, cast on 6 sts. *(14 sts)*
Row 2: Knit.
Join in pd.
Row 3: Incre, p9re, p4pd, cast on 4 sts pd. *(19 sts)*

Legs

When sewing up the legs, give them an extra pull to make them as upright as possible.

Row 4: K8pd, k11re.
Row 5: P10re, p9pd, cast on 4 sts pd. *(23 sts)*
Row 6: K13pd, k10re.
Row 7: P10re, p13pd, cast on 2 sts pd and 1 st re, with WS facing p9re from spare needle of Left Back Leg, cast on 2 sts re. *(37 sts)*
Row 8: K12re, k15pd, k10re.
Row 9: P10re, p15pd, p12re.
Row 10: K11re, k16pd, k10re.
Row 11: P10re, p16pd, p11re.
Row 12: K11re, k16pd, k10re.
Row 13: P10re, p17pd, p10re.
Row 14: K10re, k17pd, k10re.
Row 15: P11re, p17pd, p9re.
Row 16: K8re, k18pd, k6re, k2pd, k3re.
Row 17: P4re, p2pd, p5re, p18pd, p8re.
Row 18: K6re, k20pd, k4re, k1pd, k3re, k2pd, k1re.
Row 19: P1re, p3pd, p6re, p23pd, p2re, p2togre. *(36 sts)*
Row 20: K2togre, k26pd, k3re, k2pd, k3re. *(35 sts)*
Row 21: P4re, p7pd (hold 11 sts on spare needle for left neck), cast (bind) off 19 sts pd, p3pd icos, p2re (hold 5 sts on spare needle for tail).

Neck and Head

Row 1: With re and pd and with RS facing, k5re, k6pd held for neck from spare needle of Right Side of Body, then k6pd, k5re held for neck from spare needle of Left Side of Body. *(22 sts)*
Row 2: P7re, p8pd, p7re.
Row 3: K5re, k2togre, k1re, k6pd, k1re, k2togre, k5re. *(20 sts)*
Row 4: P8re, p4pd, p8re.
Row 5: K5re, k2togre, k1re, k4pd, k1re, k2togre, k5re. *(18 sts)*
Row 6: P8re, p2pd, p8re.
Row 7: K4re, k2togre, k2re, k2pd, k2re, k2togre, k4re. *(16 sts)*
Cont in re.

Row 8: Purl.
Row 9: K15, wrap and turn (leave 1 st on left-hand needle unworked; amount of unworked sts increases by 1 st on each row worked up to row 18, and then decreases by 1 st from row 19).
Row 10: P14, w&t.
Row 11: K13, w&t.
Row 12: P12, w&t.
Row 13: K11, w&t.
Row 14: P10, w&t.
Row 15: K9, w&t.
Row 16: P8, w&t.
Row 17: K7, w&t.
Row 18: P6, w&t.
Row 19: K7, w&t.
Row 20: P8, w&t.
Row 21: K9, w&t.
Row 22: P10, w&t.
Row 23: K11, w&t.
Row 24: P2, p2tog, p4, p2tog, p2, w&t. *(10 sts)*
Row 25: K11, w&t.
Row 26: P12, w&t.
Row 27: Knit across all sts. *(14 sts in total)*
Row 28: Purl.
Row 29: K2tog, k2, k2tog, k2, k2tog, k2, k2tog. *(10 sts)*
Work 7 rows st st.
Row 37: K1, loopy st 2, k4, loopy st 2, k1.
Row 38: Cast (bind) off 3 sts, k4 icos, cast (bind) off 3 sts (forms a ridge).
Rejoin re to rem sts.
Work 4 rows st st.
Cast (bind) off.

Head

The ears are sewn on at a slant to give an alert expression.

Tail

Row 1: With re and pd and with RS facing, k2re, k1pd, k2togpd held for tail from spare needle of Left Side of Body, then k2togpd, k1pd, k2re held for tail from spare needle of Right Side of Body. *(8 sts)*
Row 2: P2re, p4pd, p2re.
Row 3: K2re, k4pd, k2re.
Row 4: P3re, p2pd, p3re.
Row 5: K3re, k2pd, k3re.
Row 6: P3re, p2pd, p3re.
Row 7: K3re, k2pd, k3re.
Row 8: P1re, p2togre, p2pd, p2togre, p1re. *(6 sts)*
Row 9: K2re, k2pd, k2re.
Cont in re.
Work 5 rows st st.
Row 15: K2tog, k2, k2tog. *(4 sts)*

Row 16: [P2tog] twice. *(2 sts)*
Row 17: K2tog and fasten off.

Tummy

With re, cast on 6 sts.
Beg with a k row, work 2 rows st st.
Row 3: K2tog, k2, k2tog. *(4 sts)*
Work 11 rows st st.
Row 15: Inc, k2, inc. *(6 sts)*
Work 9 rows st st.
Row 25: Inc, k4, inc. *(8 sts)*
Work 21 rows st st.
Row 47: K2tog, k4, k2tog. *(6 sts)*
Row 48: P2tog, p2, p2tog. *(4 sts)*
Work 4 rows st st.
Row 53: Inc, k2, inc. *(6 sts)*
Work 35 rows st st.
Row 89: K2tog, k2, k2tog. *(4 sts)*
Work 5 rows st st.
Row 95: K1, loopy st 2, k1.
Row 96: Purl.
Row 97: K1, loopy st 2, k1.
Cast (bind) off.

Ear

(make 2 the same)
With re, cast on 6 sts.
Beg with a k row, work 3 rows st st.
Knit 6 rows.
Row 10: K2tog, k2, k2tog. *(4 sts)*
Knit 2 rows.
Row 13: [K2tog] twice. *(2 sts)*
Row 14: K2tog and fasten off.

Collar

With fn, cast on 26 sts.
Knit one row.
Cast (bind) off.

To Make Up

See also diagram and notes on page 173.
SEWING IN ENDS Sew in ends, leaving ends from cast on and cast (bound) off rows for sewing up.

LEGS With WS together, fold leg in half. Starting at paw, sew up leg on RS.

BODY Sew along back of dog to tail.

TAIL Cut a pipecleaner 2.5cm (1in) longer than tail. Roll a little stuffing around pipecleaner, wrap tail around pipecleaner and sew up tail on RS, sewing down to bottom of bottom. Protruding end of pipecleaner will vanish into body stuffing.

HEAD At ridge, fold down centre of nose. Sew edges of centre section to cast (bound) off rows on both sides of cheek: this makes 'box' shape for muzzle.

TUMMY Sew cast on row of tummy to bottom of dog's bottom (where back legs begin), and sew cast (bound) off row to chin. Ease and sew tummy to fit body, matching curves of tummy to legs. Leave a 2.5cm (1in) gap between front and back legs on one side.

STUFFING Pipecleaners are used to stiffen the legs and help bend them into shape. Fold a pipecleaner into a 'U' shape and measure against front two legs. Cut to approximately fit, leaving an extra 2.5cm (1in) at both ends. Fold these ends over to stop pipecleaner poking out of paws. Roll a little stuffing around pipecleaner and slip into body, one end down each front leg. Repeat with second pipecleaner and back legs. Starting at the head, stuff the dog firmly, then sew up the gap. Mould body into shape.

EARS Sew cast on row of each ear to side of dog's head. Attach at an angle sloping down towards back, so 3 sts between front of ears, 6 sts between back of ears. Catch down tip of ear with a stitch.

EYES With bl, sew 3-loop French knots positioned as in photograph.

MOUSTACHE Cut and trim loopy stitches to desired length.

NOSE With bl, embroider nose in satin stitch.

COLLAR Sew ends of collar together and pop over head.

Gun
Dogs

Weimaraner

Originally from Germany, the Weimaraner has been a popular gun dog with European royalty. A bit of a clinging vine, once a Weimaraner trusts you it won't leave your side. Untrained, it will be destructive and will eat anything in reach. Weimaraners have been muses and companions for all kinds of artists: William Wegman photographed his much-loved dog, Man Ray, and his many offspring posing in unlikely situations and even more unlikely clothes. The cover of Kate Bush's album *Hounds of Love* features Kate cuddled up with two Weimaraners. Surprising owners have included Brad Pitt and Atatürk.

Weimaraner

The Weimaraner is one of the simpler dogs to knit – just one colour and no loops.

Measurements
Length: 17cm (6¾in)
Height to top of head: 17cm (6¾in)

Materials
- Pair of 2¾mm (US 2) knitting needles
- Double-pointed 2¾mm (US 2) knitting needles (for holding stitches and for tail)
- 25g (1oz) of Rowan Kid Classic in Bitter Sweet 866 (bs)
- Small amount of Rowan Pure Wool 4ply in Eau de Nil 450 (en) for collar
- 2 pipecleaners for legs
- Tiny amount of Rowan Cashsoft 4ply in Almond 458 (al) for eyes
- 2 tiny black beads for eyes and sewing needle and black thread for sewing on
- Tiny amount of Rowan Pure Wool 4ply in Black 404 (bl) for nose

Abbreviations
See page 172.
See page 172 for I-cord Technique.
See page 172 for Wrap and Turn Method.

Right Back Leg
With bs, cast on 9 sts.
Beg with a k row, work 2 rows st st.
Row 3: Inc, k1, k2tog, k1, k2tog, k1, inc. *(9 sts)*
Row 4: Purl.
Rep rows 3–4 once more.
Row 7: K2tog, k5, k2tog.* *(7 sts)*
Work 3 rows st st.
Row 11: K2tog, inc, k1, inc, k2tog. *(7 sts)*
Row 12: Purl.
Row 13: K2tog, inc, k1, inc, k2tog. *(7 sts)*
Row 14: Purl.
Row 15: K2, inc, k1, inc, k2. *(9 sts)*
Row 16: Purl.
Row 17: K3, inc, k1, inc, k3. *(11 sts)*
Row 18: Purl.
Row 19: K4, inc, k1, inc, k4. *(13 sts)*

Head
Our Weimaraner has greeny-yellow eyes; change the colour to match your dog's eyes.

Row 20: Purl.
Row 21: K5, inc, k1, inc, k5. *(15 sts)*
Row 22: Purl.
Row 23: K6, inc, k1, inc, k6. *(17 sts)*
Row 24: Purl.
Row 25: Inc, k6, inc, k1, inc, k6, inc. *(21 sts)*
Row 26: Purl.**
Row 27: Cast (bind) off 10 sts, k to end (hold 11 sts on spare needle for Right Side of Body).

Left Back Leg

Work as for Right Back Leg to **.
Row 27: K11, cast (bind) off 10 sts (hold 11 sts on spare needle for Left Side of Body).

Right Front Leg

Work as for Right Back Leg to *.
Work 7 rows st. st.
Row 15: K2, inc, k1, inc, k2. *(9 sts)*
Row 16: Purl.
Row 17: Inc, k7, inc. *(11 sts)*
Work 5 rows st. st.***
Row 23: Cast (bind) off 5 sts, k to end (hold 6 sts on spare needle for Right Side of Body).

Left Front Leg

Work as for Right Front Leg to ***.
Row 23: K6, cast (bind) off 5 sts (hold 6 sts on spare needle for Left Side of Body).

Right Side of Body

Row 1: With bs, cast on 1 st, with RS facing k6 from spare needle of Right Front Leg, cast on 6 sts. *(13 sts)*
Row 2: Purl.
Row 3: Inc, k12, cast on 5 sts. *(19 sts)*
Row 4: Purl.
Row 5: K19, cast on 3 sts. *(22 sts)*
Row 6: Purl.
Row 7: Inc, k21, with RS facing k11 from spare needle of Right Back Leg, cast on 2 sts. *(36 sts)*
Work 9 rows st. st.
Row 17: K34, k2tog. *(35 sts)*
Row 18: P2tog, p33. *(34 sts)*
Row 19: K11, cast (bind) off 23 sts (hold 11 sts on spare needle for right neck).

Left Side of Body

Row 1: With bs, cast on 1 st, with WS facing p6 from spare needle of Left Front Leg, cast on 6 sts. *(13 sts)*
Row 2: Knit.
Row 3: Inc, p12, cast on 5 sts. *(19 sts)*
Row 4: Knit.
Row 5: P19, cast on 3 sts. *(22 sts)*
Row 6: Knit.
Row 7: Inc, p21, with WS facing p11 from spare needle of Left Back Leg, cast on 2 sts. *(36 sts)*
Work 9 rows st. st.
Row 17: P34, p2tog. *(35 sts)*
Row 18: K2tog, k33. *(34 sts)*
Row 19: P11, cast (bind) off 23 sts (hold 11 sts on spare needle for left neck).

Body

This dog has a smooth coat, so stuff the body as evenly as possible.

Neck and Head

Row 1: With bs and with RS facing, k11 held for neck from spare needle of Right Side of Body, then k11 held for neck from spare needle of Left Side of Body. *(22 sts)*

Row 2: Purl.

Row 3: K5, k2tog, k8, k2tog, k5. *(20 sts)*

Row 4: Purl.

Row 5: K5, k2tog, k6, k2tog, k5. *(18 sts)*

Row 6: Purl.

Row 7: K15, wrap and turn (leave 3 sts on left-hand needle unworked).

Row 8: Working top of head on centre 12 sts only, p12, w&t.

Row 9: K12, w&t.

Row 10: P12, w&t.

Row 11: K12, w&t.

Row 12: P12, w&t.

Row 13: Knit across all sts. *(18 sts in total)*

Work 3 rows st st.

Row 17: K15, w&t (leave 3 sts on left-hand needle unworked).

Row 18: Working top of head on centre 12 sts only, p12, w&t.

Row 19: K12, w&t.

Rep rows 18–19 once more.

Row 22: P12, w&t.

Row 23: Knit across all sts. *(18 sts in total)*

Row 24: P3, p2tog, p3, p2tog, p3, p2tog, p3. *(15 sts)*

Row 25: K4, k2tog, k3, k2tog, k4. *(13 sts)*

Row 26: P2tog, p9, p2tog. *(11 sts)*

Start jowls

Row 27: Inc, k9, inc. *(13 sts)*

Row 28: Inc, k1, p9, k1, inc. *(15 sts)*

Row 29: Inc, k1, p1, k9, p1, k1, inc. *(17 sts)*

Row 30: P3, k1, p9, k1, p3.

Row 31: K2tog, k1, p1, k9, p1, k1, k2tog. *(15 sts)*

Row 32: P2tog, k1, p9, k1, p2tog. *(13 sts)*

Row 33: K2tog, p1, k7, p1, k2tog. *(11 sts)*

Row 34: P2tog, k1, p5, k1, p2tog. *(9 sts)*

Cast (bind) off.

Tail

With two double-pointed needles and bs, cast on 8 sts.

Work in i-cord as folls:

Knit 10 rows.

Row 11: K2tog, k4, k2tog. *(6 sts)*

Work 10 rows st st.

Row 22: K2tog, k2, k2tog. *(4 sts)*

Knit 8 rows.

Row 31: [K2tog] twice. *(2 sts)*

Row 32: K2tog and fasten off.

Tummy

With bs, cast on 6 sts.

Beg with a k row, work 2 rows st st.

Row 3: K2tog, k2, k2tog. *(4 sts)*

Work 13 rows st st.

Row 17: Inc, k2, inc. *(6 sts)*

Work 27 rows st st.

Row 45: K2tog, k2, k2tog. *(4 sts)*

Work 5 rows st st.

Row 51: Inc, k2, inc. *(6 sts)*

Work 37 rows st st.

Row 89: K2tog, k2, k2tog. *(4 sts)*

Work 6 rows st st.

Cast (bind) off.

Ear

(make 2 the same)

With bs, cast on 6 sts.

Knit 10 rows.

Row 11: K2tog, k2, k2tog. *(4 sts)*

Work 2 rows st st.

Row 14: [P2tog] twice. *(2 sts)*

Row 15: K2tog and fasten off.

Collar

With en, cast on 28 sts.

Knit one row.

Cast (bind) off.

To Make Up

See also diagram and notes on page 173.

SEWING IN ENDS Sew in ends, leaving ends from cast on and cast (bound) off rows for sewing up.

LEGS With WS together, fold leg in half. Starting at paw, sew up leg on RS.

BODY Sew along back of dog and around bottom.

HEAD Fold cast (bound) off row of head in half and sew from nose to chin.

TUMMY Sew cast on row of tummy to bottom of dog's bottom (where back legs begin), and sew cast (bound) off row to chin. Ease and sew tummy to fit body. Leave a 2.5cm (1in) gap between front and back legs on one side.

STUFFING Pipecleaners are used to stiffen the legs and help bend them into shape. Fold a pipecleaner into a 'U' shape and measure against front two legs. Cut to approximately fit, leaving an extra 2.5cm (1in) at both ends. Fold these ends over to stop pipecleaner poking out of paws. Roll a little stuffing around pipecleaner and slip into body, one end down each front leg. Repeat with second pipecleaner and back legs. Starting at the head, stuff the dog firmly, then sew up the gap. Mould body into shape.

TAIL Sew cast on end of tail to dog where back meets bottom.

EARS Sew on to side of dog's head, from cast (bound) off tip to start of decrease on back edge of ear. Attach at an angle sloping down towards back, so 4 sts between tip of ears, 10 sts between back of ears. Catch front of ears down with a stitch.

EYES With al, sew 2-loop French knots positioned as in photograph. Sew beads on top of French knots.

NOSE With bl, embroider nose in satin stitch.

COLLAR Sew ends of collar together and pop over head.

Pointer

A dog on the go: as the name suggests the Pointer is always on alert and ready to hunt. Considering its muscular body and immense speed, a Pointer is happy to live indoors with families and, unusually for a dog, will cheerfully cosy up to a cat. The Pointer is thought to be the oldest breed of sporting dog and can be seen in many Renaissance paintings by artists such as Titian and Pisanello. The Pointer is also in the logo for the world-famous Westminster Dog Show in America.

Pointer

The eager Pointer has a longer than usual neck and one raised leg.

Measurements

Length: 16cm (6¼in)
Height to top of head: 16cm (6¼in)

Materials

- Pair of 2¾mm (US 2) knitting needles
- Double-pointed 2¾mm (US 2) knitting needles (for holding stitches and for tail)
- 15g (½oz) of Rowan Felted Tweed DK in Clay 177 (cl)
- 10g (¼oz) of Rowan Felted Tweed DK in Phantom 153 (ph)
- 3 pipecleaners for legs and tail
- Tiny amount of Rowan Pure Wool 4ply in Black 404 (bl) for eyes and nose

Abbreviations

See page 172.
See page 172 for Colour Knitting.
See page 172 for I-cord Technique.
See page 172 for Wrap and Turn Method.

Right Back Leg

With cl, cast on 9 sts.
Beg with a k row, work 2 rows st st.
Row 3: Inc, k1, k2tog, k1, k2tog, k1, inc. *(9 sts)*
Row 4: Purl.
Rep rows 3–4 once more.*
Join in ph.
Row 7: K2togcl, k4cl, k1ph, k2togcl. *(7 sts)*
Row 8: P3cl, p1ph, p3cl.
Row 9: K7cl.
Row 10: P2cl, p1ph, p4cl.
Row 11: K2togcl, inccl, k1cl, inccl, k2togcl. *(7 sts)*
Row 12: P7cl.
Row 13: K2togcl, inccl, k1cl, inccl, k2togcl. *(7 sts)*
Row 14: P1cl, p1ph, p5cl.
Row 15: K2cl, inccl, k1cl, inccl, k2cl. *(9 sts)*
Row 16: P3cl, p1ph, p5cl.
Row 17: K3cl, inccl, k1ph, inccl, k3cl. *(11 sts)*
Row 18: P11cl.
Row 19: K4cl, inccl, k1cl, inccl, k2cl, k1ph, k1cl. *(13 sts)*
Row 20: P4cl, p1ph, p8cl.
Row 21: K5cl, inccl, k1cl, inccl, k1cl, k1ph, k3cl. *(15 sts)*
Row 22: P15cl.
Row 23: K6cl, inccl, k1cl, inccl, k6cl. *(17 sts)*
Row 24: P1cl, p1ph, p15cl.
Row 25: Inccl, k6cl, inccl, k1cl, inccl, k1cl, k1ph, k4cl, inccl. *(21 sts)*
Row 26: P4cl, p1ph, p16cl.
Row 27: Cast (bind) off 10 sts cl, k11cl icos (hold 11 sts on spare needle for Right Side of Body).

Left Back Leg

Work as for Right Back Leg to *.
Join in ph.
Row 7: K2togcl, k1ph, k4cl, k2togcl. *(7 sts)*
Row 8: P3cl, p1ph, p3cl.
Row 9: K7cl.
Row 10: P4cl, p1ph, p2cl.
Row 11: K2togcl, inccl, k1cl, inccl, k2togcl. *(7 sts)*

Row 12: P7cl.
Row 13: K2togcl, inccl, k1cl, inccl, k2togcl. *(7 sts)*
Row 14: P5cl, p1ph, p1cl.
Row 15: K2cl, inccl, k1cl, inccl, k2cl. *(9 sts)*
Row 16: P5cl, p1ph, p3cl.
Row 17: K3cl, inccl, k1ph, inccl, k3cl. *(11 sts)*
Row 18: P11cl.
Row 19: K1cl, k1ph, k2cl, inccl, k1cl, inccl, k4cl. *(13 sts)*
Row 20: P8cl, p1ph, p4cl.
Row 21: K3cl, k1ph, k1cl, inccl, k1cl, inccl, k5cl. *(15 sts)*
Row 22: P15cl.
Row 23: K6cl, inccl, k1cl, inccl, k6cl. *(17 sts)*
Row 24: P15cl, p1ph, p1cl.
Row 25: Inccl, k4cl, k1ph, k1cl, inccl, k1cl, inccl, k6cl, inccl. *(21 sts)*
Row 26: P16cl, p1ph, p4cl.
Row 27: K11cl, cast (bind) off 10 sts cl (hold 11 sts on spare needle for Left Side of Body).

Right Front Leg

Work as for Right Back Leg to *.
Row 7: K2tog, k5, k2tog. *(7 sts)*
Row 8: Purl.
Join in ph.
Row 9: K5cl, k1ph, k1cl.
Row 10: P7cl.
Row 11: K2togcl, inccl, k1cl, inccl, k2togcl. *(7 sts)*
Row 12: Purl in cl.
Row 13: K2togcl, inccl, k1cl, inccl, k2togcl. *(7 sts)*
Row 14: P5cl, p1ph, p1cl.
Row 15: K2cl, inccl, k1cl, inccl, k2cl. *(9 sts)*
Row 16: P3cl, p1ph, p5cl.
Row 17: Inccl, k7cl, inccl. *(11 sts)*
Row 18: P2cl, p1ph, p8cl.
Row 19: Inccl, k9cl, inccl. *(13 sts)*
Row 20: P2togcl, p4cl, p1ph, p6cl. *(12 sts)*
Row 21: Cast (bind) off 6 sts cl, k6cl icos (hold 6 sts on spare needle for Right Side of Body).

Body

You need to use intarsia for the large block of colour and Fair Isle for the single or double stitches in contrast colour.

Left Front Leg

Work as for Right Back Leg to *.
Row 7: K2tog, k5, k2tog. *(7 sts)*
Row 8: Purl.
Join in ph.
Row 9: K1cl, k1ph, k5cl.
Row 10: P7cl.
Row 11: K2cl, k1ph, k4cl.
Row 12: P7cl.
Row 13: Inccl, k5cl, inccl. *(9 sts)*
Row 14: P7cl, p1ph, p1cl.
Row 15: K9cl.
Row 16: P5cl, p1ph, p3cl.
Row 17: Inccl, k7cl, inccl. *(11 sts)*
Row 18: P8cl, p1ph, p2cl.
Row 19: Inccl, k9cl, inccl. *(13 sts)*
Row 20: P6cl, p1ph, p4cl, p2togcl. *(12 sts)*
Row 21: K6cl, cast (bind) off 6 sts cl (hold 6 sts on spare needle for Left Side of Body).

Right Side of Body

Row 1: With cl, cast on 1 st, with RS facing k6 from spare needle of Right Front Leg, cast on 6 sts. *(13 sts)*
Join in ph.
Row 2: P8cl, p1ph, p4cl.
Row 3: Inccl, k8cl, k1ph, k3cl, cast on 5 sts cl. *(19 sts)*
Row 4: P11cl, p1ph, p4cl, p1ph, p2cl.
Row 5: K8cl, k1ph, k10cl, cast on 3 sts cl. *(22 sts)*
Row 6: P7cl, p1ph, p2cl, p1ph, p5cl, p1ph, p5cl.
Row 7: Inccl, k16cl, k1ph, k4cl, with RS facing k11cl from spare needle of Right Back Leg, cast on 2 sts cl. *(36 sts)*
Row 8: P13cl, p1ph, p4cl, p1ph, p6cl, p1ph, p1cl, p1ph, p3cl, p1ph, p4cl.
Row 9: K3cl, k1ph, k6cl, k2ph, k6cl, k1ph, k9cl, k1ph, k7cl.
Row 10: P1cl, p1ph, p3cl, p1ph, p10cl, p1ph, p5cl, p4ph, p2cl, p1ph, p7cl.
Row 11: K2cl, k1ph, k7cl, k6ph, k8cl, k1ph, k11cl.

Row 12: P2cl, p1ph, p4cl, p1ph, p6cl, p1ph, p4cl, p7ph, p3cl, p1ph, p6cl.
Row 13: K11cl, k7ph, k1cl, k1ph, k11cl, k1ph, k4cl.
Row 14: P10cl, p1ph, p7cl, p7ph, p6cl, p1ph, p4cl.
Row 15: K11cl, k7ph, k11cl, k1ph, k6cl.
Row 16: P14cl, p1ph, p3cl, p7ph, p3cl, p1ph, p4cl, p1ph, p2cl.
Row 17: Inccl, k7cl, k1ph, k3cl, k5ph, k8cl, k1ph, k10cl. *(37 sts)*
Row 18: P2togph, p1ph, p8cl, p1ph, p4cl, p1ph, p3cl, p4ph, p6cl, p1ph, p6cl. *(36 sts)*
Row 19: Inccl, k9cl, k1ph, k2cl, k3ph, k16cl, k2ph, k2togph. *(36 sts)*
Row 20: Cast (bind) off 4 sts ph, 15 sts cl, 3 sts ph, and 3 sts cl, p11cl icos (hold 11 sts on spare needle for right neck).

Left Side of Body

Row 1: With cl, cast on 1 st, with WS facing p6 from spare needle of Left Front Leg, cast on 6 sts. *(13 sts)*
Join in ph.
Row 2: K8cl, k1ph, k4cl.
Row 3: Inccl, p8cl, p1ph, p3cl, cast on 5 sts cl. *(19 sts)*
Row 4: K11cl, k1ph, k4cl, k1ph, k2cl.
Row 5: P8cl, p1ph, p10cl, cast on 3 sts cl. *(22 sts)*
Row 6: K7cl, k1ph, k2cl, k1ph, k5cl, k1ph, k5cl.
Row 7: Inccl, p16cl, p1ph, p4cl, with WS facing p11cl from spare needle of Left Back Leg, cast on 2 sts cl. *(36 sts)*
Row 8: K13cl, k1ph, k4cl, k1ph, k6cl, k1ph, k1cl, k1ph, k3cl, k1ph, k4cl.
Row 9: P3cl, p1ph, p6cl, p2ph, p6cl, p1ph, p9cl, p1ph, p7cl.
Row 10: K1cl, k1ph, k3cl, k1ph, k10cl, k1ph, k5cl, k4ph, k2cl, k1ph, k7cl.
Row 11: P2cl, p1ph, p7cl, p6ph, p8cl, p1ph, p11cl.

Row 12: K2cl, k1ph, k4cl, k1ph, k6cl, k1ph, k4cl, k7ph, k3cl, k1ph, k6cl.
Row 13: P11cl, p7ph, p1cl, p1ph, p11cl, p1ph, p4cl.
Row 14: K10cl, k1ph, k7cl, k7ph, k6cl, k1ph, k4cl.
Row 15: P11cl, p7ph, p11cl, p1ph, p6cl.
Row 16: K14cl, k1ph, k3cl, k7ph, k3cl, k1ph, k4cl, k1ph, k2cl.
Row 17: Inccl, p7cl, p1ph, p3cl, p5ph, p8cl, p1ph, p10cl. *(37 sts)*
Row 18: K2togph, k1ph, k8cl, k1ph, k4cl, k1ph, k3cl, k4ph, k6cl, k1ph, k6cl. *(36 sts)*
Row 19: Inccl, p9cl, p1ph, p2cl, p3ph, p16cl, p2ph, p2togph. *(36 sts)*
Row 20: Cast (bind) off 4 sts ph, 15 sts cl, 3 sts ph, and 3 sts cl, k11cl icos (hold 11 sts on spare needle for left neck).

Neck and Head

Row 1: With cl and ph and with RS facing, inccl, k2cl, k1ph, k1cl, k2togcl, k4cl held for neck from spare needle of Right Side of Body, then k4cl, k2togcl, k1cl, k1ph, k2cl, inccl held for neck from spare needle of Left Side of Body. *(22 sts)*
Row 2: P6cl, p2togph, p3cl, p1ph, p2cl, p2togcl, p1ph, p5cl. *(20 sts)*
Row 3: Inccl, k4cl, k2togcl, k4cl, k1ph, k1cl, k2togcl, k4cl, inccl. *(20 sts)*
Row 4: P4cl, p2togph, p8cl, p2togcl, p4cl. *(18 sts)*
Row 5: Incph, k1ph, k2cl, k2togcl, k1cl, k1ph, k4cl, k2togcl, k2cl, k1ph, incph. *(18 sts)*
Row 6: P4ph, p10cl, p4ph.
Row 7: K6ph, k6cl, k3ph, wrap and turn (leave 3 sts on left-hand needle unworked).
Row 8: Working top of head on centre 12 sts only, p3ph, p6cl, p3ph, w&t.
Row 9: K3ph, k3cl, k1ph, k2cl, k3ph, w&t.
Row 10: P4ph, p4cl, p4ph, w&t.
Row 11: K4ph, k1cl, k1ph, k2cl, k4ph, w&t.
Row 12: P4ph, p4cl, p4ph, w&t.

Row 13: K5ph, k2cl, k8ph. *(18 sts in total)*
Row 14: P8ph, p2cl, p8ph.
Row 15: K8ph, k2cl, k8ph.
Row 16: P8ph, p2cl, p8ph.
Row 17: K8ph, k2cl, k5ph, w&t (leave 3 sts on left-hand needle unworked).
Row 18: Working top of head on centre 12 sts only, p5ph, p2cl, p5ph, w&t.
Row 19: K5ph, k2cl, k5ph, w&t.
Rep rows 18–19 once more.
Row 22: P4ph, p4cl, p4ph, w&t.
Row 23: K3ph, k6cl, k6ph. *(18 sts in total)*
Row 24: P3ph, p2togph, p3cl, p2togcl, p3cl, p2togph, p3ph. *(15 sts)*
Row 25: K4cl, k2togcl, k3cl, k2togcl, k4cl. *(13 sts)*
Row 26: P2togcl, p4cl, p1ph, p4cl, p2togcl. *(11 sts)*
Row 27: K11cl.
Row 28: P7cl, p1ph, p3cl.
Row 29: K8cl, k1ph, k2cl.
Row 30: P5cl, p1ph, p5cl.
Row 31: K2togcl, k7cl, k2togcl. *(9 sts)*
Row 32: P9cl.
Cast (bind) off.

Tail

With two double-pointed needles and ph, cast on 6 sts.
Work in i-cord as folls:
Knit 8 rows.
Join in cl.
Row 9: K1cl, k4ph, k1cl.
Row 10: K2cl, k2ph, k2cl.
Cont in cl.
Knit 12 rows.
Row 23: K2tog, k2, k2tog. *(4 sts)*
Knit 8 rows.
Row 32: [K2tog] twice. *(2 sts)*
Row 33: K2tog and fasten off.

Tummy

With cl, cast on 6 sts.
Beg with a k row, work 2 rows st st.
Row 3: K2tog, k2, k2tog. *(4 sts)*
Work 13 rows st st.
Row 17: Inc, k2, inc. *(6 sts)*
Work 27 rows st st.
Row 45: K2tog, k2, k2tog. *(4 sts)*
Work 5 rows st st.
Row 51: Inc, k2, inc. *(6 sts)*
Work 4 rows st st.
Join in ph.
Row 56: P2cl, p1ph, p3cl.
Work 2 rows st st in cl.
Row 59: K1cl, k1ph, k4cl.
Work 3 rows st st in cl.
Row 63: K3cl, k1ph, k2cl.
Work 4 rows st st in cl.
Row 68: P3cl, p1ph, p2cl.
Work 2 rows st st in cl.
Row 71: K4cl, k1ph, k1cl.
Work 4 rows st st in cl.
Row 76: P4cl, p1ph, p1cl.
Work 3 rows st st in cl.
Row 80: P1cl, p1ph, p4cl.
Cont in cl.
Work 8 rows st st.
Row 89: K2tog, k2, k2tog. *(4 sts)*
Work 6 rows st st.
Cast (bind) off.

Ear

(make 2 the same)
With ph, cast on 6 sts.
Knit 10 rows.
Row 11: K2tog, k2, k2tog. *(4 sts)*
Knit 2 rows.
Row 14: [K2tog] twice. *(2 sts)*
Row 15: K2tog and fasten off.

To Make Up

See also diagram and notes on page 173.

SEWING IN ENDS Sew in ends, leaving ends from cast on and cast (bound) off rows for sewing up.

LEGS With WS together, fold leg in half. Starting at paw, sew up leg on RS.

BODY Sew along back of dog and around bottom.

HEAD Fold cast (bound) off row of head in half and sew from nose to chin.

TUMMY Sew cast on row of tummy to bottom of dog's bottom (where back legs begin), and sew cast (bound) off row to chin. Ease and sew tummy to fit body. Leave a 2.5cm (1in) gap between front and back legs on one side.

STUFFING Pipecleaners are used to stiffen the legs and help bend them into shape. Fold a pipecleaner into a 'U' shape and measure against front two legs. Cut to approximately fit, leaving an extra 2.5cm (1in) at both ends. Fold these ends over to stop pipecleaner poking out of paws. Roll a little stuffing around pipecleaner and slip into body, one end down each front leg. Repeat with second pipecleaner and back legs. Starting at the head, stuff the dog firmly, then sew up the gap. Mould body into shape, bending the front leg.

TAIL Cut a pipecleaner 2.5cm (1in) longer than tail. Roll a little stuffing around pipecleaner, and slip in to tail. Push protruding pipecleaner end into dog where back meets bottom and sew tail on.

EARS Sew cast on row of each ear to side of dog's head, following natural slope of head and with 7 sts between ears. Catch ears down with a stitch.

EYES With bl, sew 3-loop French knots positioned as in photograph.

NOSE With bl, embroider nose in satin stitch.

English Springer Spaniel

An excitable, energetic and useful dog, the English Springer Spaniel is used for flushing out and retrieving game birds. The Springer's nose is remarkable and its sniffing ability has been used for searching for explosives. Murphy, trained by the Prison Service, could sniff out mobile phones; so exact was his nose that he could tell the difference between the warden's and illegal phones. Braveheart Scot, William Wallace, had an English Springer Spaniel, Merlin MacDonald, that reportedly helped him to victory over the English at the Battle of Sterling Bridge.

English Springer Spaniel

The Springer Spaniel uses intarsia, Fair Isle and loopy stitch.

Measurements

Length: 20cm (8in)
Height to top of head: 15cm (6in)

Materials

- Pair of 2¾mm (US 2) knitting needles
- Double-pointed 2¾mm (US 2) knitting needles (for holding stitches)
- 20g (¾oz) of Rowan Felted Tweed DK in Clay 177 (cl)
- 10g (¼oz) of Rowan Cashsoft 4ply in Black 422 (bl)
- Small amount of Rowan Pure Wool 4ply in Mocha 417 (mo) for collar
- 2 pipecleaners for legs

Abbreviations

See page 172.
See page 172 for Colour Knitting.
See page 172 for Wrap and Turn Method.
See page 172 for Loopy Stitch. Work 2-finger loopy stitch throughout this pattern.

Right Back Leg

With cl, cast on 11 sts.
Beg with a k row, work 2 rows st st.
Row 3: Inc, k2, k2tog, k1, k2tog, k2, inc. *(11 sts)*
Row 4: Purl.
Rep rows 3–4 once more.*
Join in bl.

Row 7: K3cl, k2togcl, k1cl, k2togbl, k1bl, k2cl. *(9 sts)*
Row 8: P4cl, p1bl, p4cl.
Row 9: K9cl.
Row 10: P2cl, p1bl, p6cl.
Row 11: K9cl.
Row 12: P3cl, p1bl, p5cl.
Row 13: K3cl, inccl, k1cl, inccl, k1cl, k1bl, k1cl. *(11 sts)*
Row 14: P11cl.
Row 15: K2togcl, k2cl, inccl, k1cl, inccl, k2cl, k2togcl. *(11 sts)*
Row 16: P11cl.
Row 17: K4cl, inccl, k1cl, inccl, k1cl, k1bl, k2cl. *(13 sts)*
Row 18: P3cl, p1bl, p9cl.
Row 19: K5cl, inccl, k1cl, inccl, k3cl, k2bl. *(15 sts)*
Row 20: P3bl, p12cl.
Row 21: K6cl, inccl, k1cl, inccl, k2cl, k4bl. *(17 sts)*
Row 22: P4bl, p13cl.
Row 23: K7cl, inccl, k1cl, inccl, k2cl, k5bl. *(19 sts)*
Row 24: P5bl, p14cl.
Row 25: Cast (bind) off 9 sts cl, k5cl icos, k5bl (hold 10 sts on spare needle for Right Side of Body).

Left Back Leg

Work as for Right Back Leg to *.
Join in bl.
Row 7: K2cl, k1bl, k2togbl, k1cl, k2togcl, k3cl. *(9 sts)*
Row 8: P4cl, p1bl, p4cl.
Row 9: K9cl.
Row 10: P6cl, p1bl, p2cl.
Row 11: K9cl.
Row 12: P5cl, p1bl, p3cl.
Row 13: K1cl, k1bl, k1cl, inccl, k1cl, inccl, k3cl. *(11 sts)*
Row 14: P11cl.
Row 15: K2togcl, k2cl, inccl, k1cl, inccl, k2cl, k2togcl. *(11 sts)*

Body

When sewing up, match the curve of the tummy with the top of the legs, sewing up one side then the other.

Row 16: P11cl.
Row 17: K2cl, k1bl, k1cl, inccl, k1cl, inccl, k4cl. *(13 sts)*
Row 18: P9cl, p1bl, p3cl.
Row 19: K2bl, k3cl, inccl, k1cl, inccl, k5cl. *(15 sts)*
Row 20: P12cl, p3bl.
Row 21: K4bl, k2cl, inccl, k1cl, inccl, k6cl. *(17 sts)*
Row 22: P13cl, p4bl.
Row 23: K5bl, k2cl, inccl, k1cl, inccl, k7cl. *(19 sts)*
Row 24: P14cl, p5bl.
Row 25: K5bl, k5cl, cast (bind) off 9 sts cl (hold 10 sts on spare needle for Left Side of Body).

Right Front Leg
Work as for Right Back Leg to *.
Row 7: K3, k2tog, k1, k2tog, k3.** *(9 sts)*
Join in bl.
Row 8: P2cl, p1bl, p6cl,
Row 9: K9cl working loopy st on 2nd and 2nd-to-last stitch on first and every alt row for rest of leg.
Row 10: P4cl, p1bl, p4cl.
Row 11: K9cl.
Row 12: P9cl.
Row 13: Inccl, k4cl, k1bl, k2cl, inccl. *(11 sts)*
Row 14: P3cl, p1bl, p7cl.
Row 15: K11cl.
Row 16: P1cl, p1bl, p4cl, p1bl, p4cl.
Row 17: Inccl, k5cl, k1bl, k3cl, inccl. *(13 sts)*
Row 18: P3cl, p2bl, p8cl.
Row 19: Inccl, k5cl, k1bl, k5cl, inccl. *(15 sts)*
Row 20: P2cl, p1bl, p12cl.
Row 21: Cast (bind) off 7 sts cl, k to end in cl (hold 8 sts on spare needle for Right Side of Body).

Left Front Leg
Work as for Right Front Leg to **.
Join in bl.
Row 8: P6cl, p1bl, p2cl.

Row 9: K9cl working loopy st on 2nd and 2nd-to-last stitch on first and every alt row for rest of leg.
Row 10: P4cl, p1bl, p4cl.
Row 11: K9cl.
Row 12: P9cl.
Row 13: Inccl, k2cl, k1bl, k4cl, inccl. *(11 sts)*
Row 14: P7cl, p1bl, p3cl.
Row 15: K11cl.
Row 16: P4cl, p1bl, p4cl, p1bl, p1cl.
Row 17: Inccl, k3cl, k1bl, k5cl, inccl. *(13 sts)*
Row 18: P8cl, p2bl, p3cl.
Row 19: Inccl, k5cl, k1bl, k5cl, inccl. *(15 sts)*
Row 20: P12cl, p1bl, p2cl.
Row 21: K8cl, cast (bind) off 7 sts cl (hold 8 sts on spare needle for Left Side of Body).

Right Side of Body
Row 1: With cl, cast on 1 st, with RS facing k8 from spare needle of Right Front Leg, cast on 5 sts. *(14 sts)*
Row 2: Purl.
Join in bl.
Row 3: Inccl, k2cl, k1bl, k10cl, cast on 5 sts cl. *(20 sts)*
Row 4: P10cl, p1bl, p9cl.
Row 5: Inccl, k11cl, k1bl, k7cl, cast on 5 sts cl, with RS facing k5cl, k5bl from spare needle of Right Back Leg, cast on 2 sts bl. *(38 sts)*
Row 6: P7bl, p16cl, p1bl, p14cl.
Row 7: K3cl, k2bl, k14cl, k1bl, k11cl, k7bl.
Row 8: P7bl, p8cl, p1bl, p10cl, p1bl, p5cl, p1bl, p5cl.
Row 9: Inccl, k15cl, k3bl, k11cl, k8bl. *(39 sts)*
Row 10: P8bl, p10cl, p5bl, p5cl, p1bl, p10cl,
Row 11: K4cl, k1bl, k11cl, k6bl, k9cl, k8bl.
Row 12: P8bl, p9cl, p5bl, p5cl, p1bl, p11cl.
Row 13: K2cl, k2bl, k13cl, k6bl, k8cl, k8bl.
Row 14: P8bl, p7cl, p7bl, p12cl, p4bl, p1cl.
Row 15: K5bl, k3cl, k1bl, k9cl, k6bl, k7cl, k8bl.
Row 16: P8bl, p3cl, p1bl, p3cl, p5bl, p9cl, p1bl, p3cl, p6bl.

Row 17: K7bl, k13cl, k4bl, k2cl, k3bl, k2cl, k6bl, k2togbl. *(38 sts)*
Row 18: Cast (bind) off 9 sts bl, p8bl icos, p8cl, p1bl, p4cl, p8bl. *(29 sts)*
Row 19: K10bl, k3cl, k1bl, k3cl, k1bl, k4cl, k7bl.
Row 20: Cast (bind) off 6 sts bl and 3 sts cl, p8cl icos, p12bl. *(20 sts)*
Row 21: K13bl, k7cl.
Row 22: Cast (bind) off 7 sts cl and 2 sts bl, p11bl icos (hold 11 sts on spare for right neck).

Left Side of Body
Row 1: With cl, cast on 1 st, with WS facing p8 from spare needle of Left Front Leg, cast on 5 sts. *(14 sts)*
Row 2: Knit.
Join in bl.
Row 3: Inccl, p2cl, p1bl, p10cl, cast on 5 sts cl. *(20 sts)*
Row 4: K10cl, k1bl, k9cl.
Row 5: Inccl, p11cl, p1bl, p7cl, cast on 5 sts cl, with WS facing p5cl, p5bl from spare needle of Left Back Leg, cast on 2 sts bl. *(38 sts)*
Row 6: K7bl, k16cl, k1bl, k14cl.
Row 7: P3cl, p2bl, p14cl, p1bl, p11cl, p7bl.
Row 8: K7bl, k8cl, k1bl, k10cl, k1bl, k5cl, k1bl, k5cl.
Row 9: Inccl, p15cl, p3bl, p11cl, p8bl. *(39 sts)*
Row 10: K8bl, k10cl, k5bl, k5cl, k1bl, k10cl.
Row 11: P4cl, p1bl, p11cl, p6bl, p9cl, p8bl.
Row 12: K8bl, k9cl, k5bl, k5cl, k1bl, k11cl.
Row 13: P2cl, p2bl, p13cl, p6bl, p8cl, p8bl.
Row 14: K8bl, k7cl, k7bl, k12cl, k4bl, k1cl.
Row 15: P5bl, p3cl, p1bl, p9cl, p6bl, p7cl, p8bl.
Row 16: K8bl, k3cl, k1bl, k3cl, k5bl, k9cl, k1bl, k3cl, k6bl.
Row 17: P7bl, p13cl, p4bl, p2cl, p3bl, p2cl, p6bl, p2togbl. *(38 sts)*
Row 18: Cast (bind) off 9 sts bl, k8bl icos, k8cl, k1bl, k4cl, k8bl. *(29 sts)*

Row 19: P10bl, p3cl, p1bl, p3cl, p1bl, p4cl, p7bl.

Row 20: Cast (bind) off 6 sts bl and 3 sts cl, k8cl icos, k12bl. *(20 sts)*

Row 21: P13bl, p7cl.

Row 22: Cast (bind) off 7 sts cl and 2 sts bl, k11bl icos (hold 11 sts on spare needle for left neck).

Neck and Head

Row 1: With bl and with RS facing, k11 held for neck from spare needle of Right Side of Body, then k11 held for neck from spare needle of Left Side of Body. *(22 sts)*

Row 2: P6, p2tog, p6, p2tog, p6. *(20 sts)*

Row 3: Inc, k4, k2tog, k6, k2tog, k4, inc. *(20 sts)*

Row 4: Purl.

Ears

The loopy stitch ears can be caught down with a sewn stitch if they are too flyaway.

Row 5: K5, k2tog, k6, k2tog, k5. *(18 sts)*

Row 6: Purl.

Row 7: K15, wrap and turn (leave 3 sts on left-hand needle unworked).

Row 8: Working top of head on centre 12 sts only, p12, w&t.

Row 9: K12, w&t.

Rep rows 8–9 once more.

Row 12: P12, w&t.

Row 13: Knit across all sts. *(18 sts in total)*

Row 14: Purl.

Join in cl.

Row 15: K8bl, k2cl, k8bl.

Row 16: P8bl, p2cl, p8bl.

Row 17: K8bl, k2cl, k5bl, w&t (leave 3 sts on left-hand needle unworked).

Row 18: Working top of head on centre 12 sts only, p5bl, p2cl, p5bl, w&t.

Row 19: K5bl, k2cl, k5bl, w&t.

Row 20: P5bl, p2cl, p5bl, w&t.

Rep rows 19–20 once more.

Row 23: P4bl, p4cl, p4bl, w&t.

Row 24: K3bl, k6cl, k6bl. *(18 sts in total)*

Row 25: P2bl, p2togbl, p4cl, p2togcl, p4cl, p2togbl, p2bl. *(15 sts)*

Row 26: K4cl, k2togcl, k3cl, k2togcl, k4cl. *(13 sts)*

Row 27: P4cl, p1bl, p8cl.

Row 28: K3cl, k1bl, k3cl, k1bl, k3cl, k1bl, k1cl.

Row 29: P7cl, p1bl, p3cl, p1bl, p1cl.

Row 30: K8cl, k1bl, k4cl.

Row 31: P3cl, p2togcl, p3cl, p2togcl, p3cl. *(11 sts)*

Row 32: K2cl, k1bl, k6cl, k1bl, k1cl.

Row 33: P2togcl, p1cl, p1bl, p2cl, p1bl, p2cl, p2togcl. *(9 sts)*

Row 34: K9cl.

Cast (bind) off.

Tail

With bl, cast on 6 sts.

Beg with a k row, work 8 rows st st.

Cast (bind) off.

Tummy

With cl, cast on 6 sts.

Beg with a k row, work 2 rows st st.

Row 3: K2tog, k2, k2tog. *(4 sts)*

Work 11 rows st st.

Row 15: Inc, k2, inc. *(6 sts)*

Work 3 rows st st.

Row 19: K1, loopy st 1, k2, loopy st 1, k1.

Row 20: Purl.

Rep rows 19–20, 11 times more.

Row 43: K2tog, k2, k2tog. *(4 sts)*

Work 5 rows st st.

Row 49: Inc, k2, inc. *(6 sts)*

Work 3 rows st st.

Row 53: K1, loopy st 1, k2, loopy st 1, k1.

Row 54: Purl

Rep rows 53–54, 5 times more.

Work 14 rows st st.

Row 79: K2tog, k2, k2tog. *(4 sts)*

Work 7 rows st st.

Cast (bind) off.

Ear

(make 2 the same)

With bl, cast on 4 sts.

Beg with a k row, work 2 rows st st.

Row 3: Inc, loopy st 2, inc. *(6 sts)*

Row 4: Purl.

Row 5: K1, loopy st 4, k1.

Row 6: Purl.

Rep rows 5–6 twice more.

Row 11: K2, loopy st 2, k2.

Row 12: Purl.

Rep rows 11–12 once more.

Row 15: K2tog, loopy st 2, k2tog. *(4 sts)*

Row 16: Purl.

Rep rows 15–16 once more.

Cast (bind) off.

Collar

With mo, cast on 26 sts.
Knit one row.
Cast (bind) off.

To Make Up

See also diagram and notes on page 173.

SEWING IN ENDS Sew in ends, leaving ends
from cast on and cast (bound) off rows for
sewing up.

LEGS With WS together, fold leg in half.
Starting at paw, sew up leg on RS.

BODY Sew along back of dog and around
bottom.

HEAD Fold cast (bound) off row of head in
half and sew from nose to chin.

TUMMY Sew cast on row of tummy to
bottom of dog's bottom (where back legs
begin), and sew cast (bound) off row to chin.
Ease and sew tummy to fit body. Leave a
2.5cm (1in) gap between front and back legs
on one side.

STUFFING Pipecleaners are used to stiffen
the legs and help bend them into shape. Fold
a pipecleaner into a 'U' shape and measure
against front two legs. Cut to approximately
fit, leaving an extra 2.5cm (1in) at both ends.
Fold these ends over to stop pipecleaner
poking out of paws. Roll a little stuffing
around pipecleaner and slip into body, one
end down each front leg. Repeat with second
pipecleaner and back legs. Starting at the
head, stuff the dog firmly, then sew up the
gap. Mould body into shape.

TAIL Sew up tail on RS and sew to dog
where back meets bottom.

EARS Sew cast on row of each ear to side of
dog's head, following natural slope of head
and with 6 sts between ears.

EYES With bl, sew 3-loop French knots
positioned as in photograph.

NOSE With bl, embroider nose in satin stitch.

COLLAR Sew ends of collar together and
pop over head.

Golden Retriever

Handsome, multi-talented, highly intelligent, yet placid and amiable, the Golden Retriever is the George Clooney of the dog world. Bred in the 1800s by Lord Tweedmouth, Retrievers were a cross between retrieving dogs and water spaniels, but can now work in almost any field, from search and rescue to guiding the blind and deaf. Peter Mandelson, Ricky Martin and Dmitry Medvedev all own Golden Retrievers.

Golden Retriever

The Golden Retriever is made in smooth yarn that loops beautifully.

Measurements

Length: 20cm (8in)
Height to top of head: 18cm (7in)

Materials

- Pair of 2¾mm (US 2) knitting needles
- Double-pointed 2¾mm (US 2) knitting needles (for holding stitches)
- 30g (1¼oz) of Rowan Creative Focus Worsted in Camel 02132 (ca)
- Small amount of Rowan Cashsoft 4ply in Toxic 459 (tx) for collar
- 2 pipecleaners for legs
- Tiny amount of Rowan Pure Wool 4ply in Black 404 (bl) for eyes and nose

Abbreviations

See page 172.
See page 172 for Wrap and Turn Method.
See page 172 for Loopy Stitch. Work 2-finger loopy stitch throughout this pattern.

Right Back Leg

With ca, cast on 7 sts.
Beg with a k row, work 2 rows st st.
Row 3: Inc, k2tog, k1, k2tog, inc. *(7 sts)*
Work 7 rows st st.
Row 11: K1, inc, k1, inc, k1, inc, k1. *(10 sts)*
Row 12 and every alt row: Purl.
Row 13: K2tog, inc, loopy st 1, k2, loopy st 1, inc, k2tog. *(10 sts)*
Row 15: K2, [inc] twice, k2, [inc] twice, k2. *(14 sts)*
Row 17: K1, loopy st 1, k1, [inc] twice, k4, [inc] twice, k1, loopy st 1, k1. *(18 sts)*
Row 19: K3, inc, k10, inc, k3. *(20 sts)*
Row 21: K1, loopy st 1, k1, inc, k12, inc, k1, loopy st 1, k1. *(22 sts)*
Row 23: K3, inc, k14, inc, k3. *(24 sts)*
Row 25: K1, loopy st 1, k20, loopy st 1, k1.*
Row 27: Cast (bind) off 12 sts, k to end (hold 12 sts on spare needle for Right Side of Body).

Left Back Leg

Work as for Right Back Leg to *.
Row 26: Purl.
Row 27: K12, cast (bind) off 12 sts (hold 12 sts on spare needle for Left Side of Body).

Right Front Leg

With ca, cast on 7 sts.
Beg with a k row, work 2 rows st st.
Row 3: Inc, k2tog, k1, k2tog, inc. *(7 sts)*
Work 3 rows st st.
Row 7: Inc, k5, inc. *(9 sts)*
Work 3 rows st st.
Row 11: K1, loopy st 1, k5, loopy st 1, k1.
Work 3 rows st st.
Row 15: K1, loopy st 1, k5, loopy st 1, k1.
Work 3 rows st st.
Row 19: Inc, loopy st 1, k5, loopy st 1, inc. *(11 sts)*
Row 20: Purl.**
Row 21: Cast (bind) off 5 sts, k to end (hold 6 sts on spare needle for Right Side of Body).

Tail

The Retriever has quite a muscular tail as it's a great wagger.

Left Front Leg

Work as for Right Front Leg to **.
Row 21: K6, cast (bind) off 5 sts (hold 6 sts on spare needle for Left Side of Body).

Right Side of Body

Row 1: With ca, cast on 1 st, with RS facing k6 from spare needle of Right Front Leg, cast on 3 sts. *(10 sts)*
Row 2: Purl.
Row 3: K10, cast on 4 sts. *(14 sts)*
Row 4: Purl.
Row 5: Inc, k13, cast on 3 sts. *(18 sts)*
Row 6: Purl.
Row 7: K18, cast on 4 sts. *(22 sts)*
Row 8: Purl.
Row 9: K22, with RS facing k12 from spare needle of Right Back Leg. *(34 sts)*
Work 5 rows st st.
Row 15: K32, k2tog. *(33 sts)*
Row 16: Purl.
Row 17: K31, k2tog. *(32 sts)*
Row 18: Purl.
Row 19: K30, k2tog. *(31 sts)*
Row 20: Purl.
Row 21: K29, k2tog. *(30 sts)*
Row 22: Cast (bind) off 21 sts, p to end (hold 9 sts on spare needle for right neck).

Left Side of Body

Row 1: With ca, cast on 1 st, with WS facing p6 from spare needle of Left Front Leg, cast on 3 sts. *(10 sts)*
Row 2: Knit.
Row 3: P10, cast on 4 sts. *(14 sts)*
Row 4: Knit.
Row 5: Inc, p13, cast on 3 sts. *(18 sts)*
Row 6: Knit.
Row 7: P18, cast on 4 sts. *(22 sts)*
Row 8: Knit.
Row 9: P22, with WS facing p12 from spare needle of Left Back Leg. *(34 sts)*
Work 5 rows st st.
Row 15: P32, p2tog. *(33 sts)*

Row 16: Knit.
Row 17: P31, p2tog. *(32 sts)*
Row 18: Knit.
Row 19: P30, p2tog. *(31 sts)*
Row 20: Knit.
Row 21: P29, p2tog. *(30 sts)*
Row 22: Cast (bind) off 21 sts, k to end (hold 9 sts on spare needle for left neck).

Neck and Head

Row 1: With ca and with RS facing, k9 held for neck from spare needle of Right Side of Body, then k9 held for neck from spare needle of Left Side of Body. *(18 sts)*
Row 2: Purl.
Row 3: Knit.
Row 4: Purl.
Row 5: Inc, k16, inc. *(20 sts)*
Row 6: Purl.
Row 7: K17, wrap and turn (leave 3 sts on left-hand needle unworked).
Row 8: Working top of head on centre 14 sts only, p14, w&t.
Row 9: K14, w&t.
Row 10: P14, w&t.
Row 11: K14, w&t.
Row 12: P14, w&t.
Row 13: Knit across all sts. *(20 sts in total)*
Work 3 rows st st.
Row 17: K16, w&t (leave 4 sts on left-hand needle unworked).
Row 18: Working top of head on centre 12 sts only, p12, w&t.
Row 19: K12, w&t.
Row 20: P12, w&t.
Row 21: K12, w&t.
Row 22: P12, w&t.
Row 23: Knit across all sts. *(20 sts in total)*
Row 24: Purl.
Row 25: K4, [k2tog twice, k4, [k2tog] twice, k4. *(16 sts)*
Row 26: Purl.
Row 27: K4, k2tog, k4, k2tog, k4. *(14 sts)*
Row 28: Purl.

Row 29: K3, k2tog, k4, k2tog, k3. *(12 sts)*
Work 3 rows st st.
Row 33: K2tog, k8, k2tog. *(10 sts)*
Row 34: Purl.
Cast (bind) off.

Tail

With ca, cast on 1 st.
Row 1: Inc. *(2 sts)*
Row 2: Purl.
Row 3: [Inc] twice. *(4 sts)*
Row 4: Purl.
Row 5: K1, inc, k2. *(5 sts)*
Row 6: Purl.
Row 7: K2, loopy st 1, k2.
Row 8: Purl.
Row 9: Knit.
Row 10: Purl.
Rep rows 7–10 twice more.
Row 19: Inc, k1, loopy st 1, k1, inc. *(7 sts)*
Work 3 rows st st.
Row 23: K3, loopy st 1, k3.
Row 24: Purl.
Row 25: Knit.
Row 26: Purl.
Rep rows 23–26 once more.
Row 31: K3, loopy st 1, k3.
Row 32: Purl.
Cast (bind) off.

Head

Stuff the nose carefully so there is a nice curve to the chin.

Tummy

With ca, cast on 1 st.
Row 1: Inc. *(2 sts)*
Row 2: [Inc] twice. *(4 sts)*
Row 3: Inc, k2, inc. *(6 sts)*
Row 4: Inc, p4, inc. *(8 sts)*
Work 18 rows st st.
Row 23: K3, loopy st 2, k3.
Row 24: Purl.
Row 25: Knit.
Row 26: Purl.
Rep rows 23–26, 6 times more.
Row 51: K1, loopy st 6, k1.
Row 52: Purl.
Row 53: Knit.
Row 54: Purl.
Rep rows 51–54 once more.
Row 59: K2tog, loopy st 4, k2tog. *(6 sts)*
Work 3 rows st st.
Row 63: K1, loopy st 4, k1.
Work 15 rows st st.

Row 79: K2tog, k2, k2tog. *(4 sts)*
Work 11 rows st st.
Row 91: [K2tog] twice. *(2 sts)*
Row 92: Purl.
Row 93: K2tog and fasten off.

Ear

(make 2 the same)
With ca, cast on 7 sts.
Beg with a k row, work 5 rows st st.
Row 6: P2tog, p3, p2tog. *(5 sts)*
Row 7: K2tog, k1, k2tog. *(3 sts)*
Row 8: Purl.
Row 9: K3tog and fasten off.

Collar

With tx, cast on 30 sts.
Knit one row.
Cast (bind) off.

To Make Up

See also diagram and notes on page 173.

SEWING IN ENDS Sew in ends, leaving ends from cast on and cast (bound) off rows for sewing up.

LEGS With WS together, fold leg in half. Starting at paw, sew up leg on RS.

BODY Sew along back of dog and 2cm (¾in) down bottom.

HEAD Fold cast (bound) off row of head in half and sew from nose to chin.

TUMMY Sew cast on row of tummy to where you have finished sewing down bottom, and sew cast (bound) off row to chin. Ease and sew tummy to fit body. Leave a 2.5cm (1in) gap between front and back legs on one side.

STUFFING Pipecleaners are used to stiffen the legs and help bend them into shape. Fold a pipecleaner into a 'U' shape and measure against front two legs. Cut to approximately fit, leaving an extra 2.5cm (1in) at both ends. Fold these ends over to stop pipecleaner poking out of paws. Roll a little stuffing around pipecleaner and slip into body, one end down each front leg. Repeat with second pipecleaner and back legs. Starting at the head, stuff the dog firmly, then sew up the gap. Mould body into shape.

TAIL Sew up tail on RS and sew to dog where back meets bottom, with loops on underside.

EARS Sew cast on row of each ear to side of dog's head, with wrong side of ears facing downwards. Attach at an angle sloping down towards back, so 6 sts between front of ears, 10 sts between back of ears.

EYES With bl, sew 2-loop French knots with 1 tiny straight stitch on the outside, positioned as in photograph.

NOSE With bl, embroider nose in satin stitch.

COLLAR Sew ends of collar together and pop over head.

Working

Irish Wolfhound

The Irish Wolfhound is one of the largest breeds of dog, reaching the size of a small pony. Originally bred in Ireland to...hunt wolves, since the last wolf in Ireland was killed in 1786, they now make excellent guard dogs and friendly and affectionate, if rather large, family pets. They are also much in demand as regimental mascots. The playwright Edward Albee, author of *Who's Afraid of Virginia Woolf?*, coincidentally kept Wolfhounds called Samantha, Jane, Jennifer, Harold and Andrew.

Irish Wolfhound

The Irish Wolfhound is knitted in wool and mohair yarns to give a slightly rough coat.

Measurements

Length: 20cm (8in)
Height to top of head: 18cm (7in)

Materials

- Pair of 2¾mm (US 2) knitting needes
- Double-pointed 2¾mm (US 2) knitting needles (for holding stitches)
- 20g (¾oz) of Rowan Cashsoft 4ply in Thunder 437 (th)
- 20g (¾oz) of Rowan Kidsilk Haze in Smoke 605 (sm)
- NOTE: use one strand of th and one strand of sm held together, and this is called ths
- Small amount of Rowan Cashsoft 4ply in Redwood 429 (re) for collar
- 3 pipecleaners for legs and tail
- Tiny amount of Rowan Pure Wool 4ply in Black 404 (bl) for eyes and nose
- 2 tiny black beads for eyes and sewing needle and black thread for sewing on

Abbreviations

See page 172.
See page 172 for Wrap and Turn Method.
See page 172 for Loopy Stitch. Work 2-finger loopy stitch throughout this pattern; knit the sts before and after the loop in ths, but make the loop using one strand of sm only.

Right Back Leg

With ths, cast on 6 sts.
Beg with a k row, work 2 rows st st.
Row 3: Inc, k1, k2tog, k1, inc. *(7 sts)*
Row 4: Purl.
Row 5: Inc, k2tog, k1, k2tog, inc. *(7 sts)*
Work 5 rows st st.
Row 11: K2tog, [inc] 3 times, k2tog. *(8 sts)*
Row 12: Purl.
Row 13: K2tog, [inc] 4 times, k2tog. *(10 sts)*
Row 14: Purl.
Row 15: K2tog, [inc] twice, k2, [inc] twice, k2tog. *(12 sts)*
Row 16: Purl.
Row 17: [Inc] twice, k8, [inc] twice. *(16 sts)*
Row 18: Purl.
Row 19: Inc, k14, inc. *(18 sts)*
Row 20: Purl.
Row 21: Inc, k16, inc. *(20 sts)*
Row 22: Purl.
Row 23: Inc, k18, inc. *(22 sts)*
Row 24: Purl.*
Row 25: Cast (bind) off 11 sts, k to end (hold 11 sts on spare needle for Right Side of Body).

Left Back Leg

Work as for Right Back Leg to *.
Row 25: K11, cast (bind) off 11 sts (hold 11 sts on spare needle for Left Side of Body).

Right Front Leg

With ths, cast on 6 sts.
Beg with a k row, work 2 rows st st.
Row 3: Inc, [k2tog] twice, inc. *(6 sts)*
Row 4: Purl.
Row 5: K2, [inc] twice, k2. *(8 sts)*
Work 7 rows st st.
Row 13: K1, inc, k4, inc, k1. *(10 sts)*
Row 14: Purl.
Work 2 rows st st.
Row 17: K1, inc, k6, inc, k1. *(12 sts)*
Row 18: Purl.
Row 19: K1, inc, k8, inc, k1. *(14 sts)*

Tail

The Wolfhound's tail is knitted separately and stuffed with a pipecleaner so you can bend it into shape.

Row 20: Purl.
Row 21: K1, inc, k10, inc, k1. *(16 sts)*
Row 22: Purl.**
Row 23: Cast (bind) off 8 sts, k to end (hold 8 sts on spare needle for Right Side of Body).

Left Front Leg

Work as for Right Front leg to **.
Row 23: K8, cast (bind) off 8 sts (leave 8 sts on spare needle for Left Side of Body).

Right Side of Body

Row 1: With ths, cast on 1 st, with RS facing k8 from spare needle of Right Front Leg, cast on 6 sts. *(15 sts)*
Row 2: Purl.
Row 3: K15, cast on 8 sts. *(23 sts)*
Row 4: Purl.
Row 5: K23, cast on 4 sts. *(27 sts)*
Row 6: Purl.
Row 7: K27, with RS facing k11 from spare needle of Right Back Leg. *(38 sts)*
Work 3 rows st st.
Row 11: Inc, k37. *(39 sts)*
Work 7 rows st st.
Row 19: K37, k2tog. *(38 sts)*
Row 20: Purl.
Row 21: K2tog, k34, k2tog. *(36 sts)*
Row 22: Purl.
Row 23: K34, k2tog. *(35 sts)*
Row 24: P35.
Row 25: K10, cast (bind) off 25 sts (hold 10 sts on spare needle for right neck).

Left Side of Body

Row 1: With ths, cast on 1 st, with WS facing p8 from spare needle of Left Front Leg, cast on 6 sts. *(15 sts)*
Row 2: Knit.
Row 3: P15, cast on 8 sts. *(23 sts)*
Row 4: Knit.
Row 5: P23, cast on 4 sts. *(27 sts)*
Row 6: Knit.

Row 7: P27, with WS facing p11 from spare needle of Left Back Leg. *(38 sts)*
Work 3 rows st st.
Row 11: Inc, p37. *(39 sts)*
Work 7 rows st st.
Row 19: P37, p2tog. *(38 sts)*
Row 20: Knit.
Row 21: P2tog, p34, p2tog. *(36 sts)*
Row 22: Knit.
Row 23: P34, p2tog. *(35 sts)*
Row 24: K35
Row 25: P10, cast (bind) off 25 sts (hold 10 sts on spare needle for left neck),

Neck and Head

Row 1: With ths and with RS facing, k10 held for neck from spare needle of Right Side of Body, then k10 held for neck from spare needle of Left Side of Body. *(20 sts)*
Row 2: P9, p2tog, p9. *(19 sts)*
Row 3: Knit.
Row 4: P2tog, p15, p2tog. *(17 sts)*
Work 4 rows st st.
Row 9: K2tog, k13, k2tog. *(15 sts)*
Row 10: Purl.
Row 11: K12, wrap and turn (leave 3 sts on left-hand needle unworked).
Row 12: Working top of head on centre 9 sts only, p9, w&t.
Row 13: K9, w&t.
Row 14: P9, w&t.
Row 15: K9, w&t.
Row 16: P9, w&t.
Row 17: Knit across all sts. *(15 sts in total)*
Work 3 rows st st.
Row 21: K12, w&t (leave 3 sts on left-hand needle unworked).
Row 22: Working top of head on centre 9 sts only, p9, w&t.
Row 23: K1, loopy st 1, k5, loopy st 1, k1.
Row 24: P9, w&t.
Row 25: K9, w&t.
Row 26: P9, w&t.
Row 27: Knit across all sts. *(15 sts in total)*

Neck

If the neck seems too big, reduce the number of stitches on the collar; this will pull it in.

Row 28: Purl.
Row 29: K4, loopy st 1, k5, loopy st 1, k4.
Row 30: Purl.
Row 31: K4, loopy st 1, k5, loopy st 1, k4.
Row 32: Purl.
Row 33: K5, loopy st 1, k3, loopy st 1, k5.
Row 34: Purl.
Row 35: K5, loopy st 1, k3, loopy st 1, k5.
Row 36: Purl.
Row 37: K5, loopy st 1, k3, loopy st 1, k5.
Row 38: P2tog, p11, p2tog. *(13 sts)*
Cast (bind) off.

Tail

With ths, cast on 9 sts.
Beg with a k row, work 8 rows st st.
Row 9: K2tog, k5, k2tog. *(7 sts)*
Work 7 rows st st.
Row 17: K2tog, k3, k2tog. *(5 sts)*
Work 9 rows st st.
Row 27: K2tog, k1, k2tog. *(3 sts)*
Work 11 rows st st.
Row 39: K2tog, k1. *(2 sts)*
Row 40: P2tog and fasten off.

Tummy

With ths, cast on 2 sts.
Row 1: [Inc] twice. *(4 sts)*
Row 2: Purl.
Row 3: Inc, k2, inc. *(6 sts)*
Row 4: Purl.
Row 5: Inc, k4, inc. *(8 sts)*
Row 6: Purl.
Row 7: Inc, k6, inc. *(10 sts)*
Row 8: Purl.
Work 10 rows st st.
Row 19: K1, loopy st 1, k6, loopy st 1, k1.
Row 20: Purl.
Row 21: Knit.
Row 22: Purl.
Rep rows 19–22, 8 times more.
Row 55: K2tog, loopy st 1, k4, loopy st 1, k2tog. *(8 sts)*

Work 3 rows st st.
Row 59: K1, loopy st 1, k4, loopy st 1, k1.
Work 3 rows st st.
Row 63: K2tog, loopy st 1, k2, loopy st 1, k2tog. *(6 sts)*
Work 3 rows st st.
Row 67: K1, loopy st 1, k2, loopy st 1, k1.
Row 68: Purl.
Row 69: Knit.
Row 70: Purl.
Rep rows 67–70, 3 times more.
Row 83: K2tog, loopy st 1, k1, k2tog. *(4 sts)*
Work 3 rows st st.
Cast (bind) off.

Ear

(make 2 the same)
With ths, cast on 7 sts.
Beg with a k row, work 4 rows st st.
Row 5: K2tog, k3, k2tog. *(5 sts)*
Row 6: Purl.
Row 7: K2tog, k1, k2tog. *(3 sts)*
Row 8: Purl.
Cast (bind) off 3 sts.

Collar

With re, cast on 30 sts.
Knit one row.
Cast (bind) off.

To Make Up

See also diagram and notes on page 173.
SEWING IN ENDS Sew in ends, leaving ends from cast on and cast (bound) off rows for sewing up.
LEGS With WS together, fold leg in half. Starting at paw, sew up leg on RS.
BODY Sew along back of dog and around bottom.
HEAD Fold cast (bound) off row of head in half and sew from nose to chin.
TUMMY Sew cast on row of tummy to top of dog's bottom (where back meets top of

bottom), and sew cast (bound) off row to chin. Ease and sew tummy to fit body. Leave a 2.5cm (1in) gap between front and back legs on one side.

STUFFING Pipecleaners are used to stiffen the legs and help bend them into shape. Fold a pipecleaner into a 'U' shape and measure against front two legs. Cut to approximately fit, leaving an extra 2.5cm (1in) at both ends. Fold these ends over to stop pipecleaner poking out of paws. Roll a little stuffing around pipecleaner and slip into body, one end down each front leg. Repeat with second pipecleaner and back legs. Starting at the head, stuff the dog firmly, then sew up the gap. Mould body into shape.

TAIL Cut a pipecleaner 2.5cm (1in) longer than tail. Roll a little stuffing around pipecleaner, wrap tail around pipecleaner and sew up tail on RS. Push protruding pipecleaner end into dog where back meets bottom and sew tail on.

EARS Sew cast on row of each ear to side of dog's head, with wrong side of ears facing downwards. Attach at an angle sloping down towards nose, so 4 sts between front of ears, 2 sts between back of ears.

EYES With bl, sew 2-loop French knots positioned as in photograph. Sew beads on top of French knots.

NOSE With bl, embroider nose in satin stitch.

COLLAR Sew ends of collar together and pop over head.

LOOPS Cut all loops and trim as desired.

Beagle

An ancient breed, the Beagle is a scent hound, used for sniffing out rabbits and hares. Its ancestors were brought to England by William the Conqueror. Unfortunately, due to their placid nature Beagles used to be often used in animal testing. Fortunately for the easy-going Beagle, these days they are more likely to be a family pet. Butch the Beagle held the Guinness World Record for oldest dog, dying in 2003 aged 28 (196 in human years). Notorious Beagles include one we have known – Dee, a dog with a mission – and the most famous Beagle of all, Snoopy from the *Peanuts* cartoon.

Beagle

The Beagle is a neat little dog, so make yours stand up very straight, with the tail bending over slightly.

Measurements

Length: 17cm (6¾in)
Height to top of head: 15cm (6in)

Materials

- Pair of 2¾mm (US 2) knitting needles
- Double-pointed 2¾mm (US 2) knitting needles (for holding stitches)
- 15g (½oz) of Rowan Pure Wool 4ply in Snow 412 (sn)
- 10g (¼oz) of Rowan Pure Wool 4ply in Ochre 461 (oc)
- 10g (¼oz) of Rowan Pure Wool 4ply in Black 404 (bl)
- Small amount of Rowan Cashsoft 4ply in Bluebottle 449 (bb) for collar
- 3 pipecleaners for legs and tail

Abbreviations

See page 172.
See page 172 for Colour Knitting.
See page 172 for Wrap and Turn Method.

Right Back Leg

With sn, cast on 11 sts.
Beg with a k row, work 2 rows st st.
Row 3: Inc, k2, k2tog, k1, k2tog, k2, inc. *(11 sts)*
Row 4: Purl.
Rep rows 3–4 once more.
Row 7: K2tog, k7, k2tog.* *(9 sts)*
Work 3 rows st st.
Row 11: K2tog, k1, inc, k1, inc, k1, k2tog. *(9 sts)*
Row 12: Purl.
Rep rows 11–12 once more.
Row 15: K3, inc, k1, inc, k3. *(11 sts)*
Row 16: Purl.**
Join in oc.
Row 17: K4sn, incsn, k1sn, incsn, k2sn, k2oc. *(13 sts)*
Row 18: P2oc, p11sn.
Row 19: K5sn, incsn, k1sn, incsn, k2sn, k3oc. *(15 sts)*
Row 20: P3oc, p12sn.
Row 21: K6sn, incsn, k1sn, incsn, k3sn, k3oc. *(17 sts)*
Row 22: P4oc, p13sn.
Row 23: K7sn, incsn, k1sn, incsn, k3sn, k4oc. *(19 sts)*
Row 24: P4oc, p15sn.
Row 25: Cast (bind) off 9 sts sn, k6sn icos, k4oc (hold 10 sts on spare needle for Right Side of Body).

Left Back Leg

Work as for Right Back Leg to **.
Join in oc.
Row 17: K2oc, k2sn, incsn, k1sn, incsn, k4sn. *(13 sts)*
Row 18: P11sn, p2oc.
Row 19: K3oc, k2sn, incsn, k1sn, incsn, k5sn. *(15 sts)*
Row 20: P12sn, p3oc.
Row 21: K3oc, k3sn, incsn, k1sn, incsn, k6sn. *(17 sts)*
Row 22: P13sn, p4oc.

Row 23: K4oc, k3sn, incsn, k1sn, incsn, k7sn. *(19 sts)*
Row 24: P15sn, p4oc.
Row 25: K4oc, k6sn, cast (bind) off 9 sts sn (hold 10 sts on spare needle for Left Side of Body).

Right Front Leg

Work as for Right Back Leg to *.
Work 7 rows st st.
Join in oc.
Row 15: Incsn, k4sn, k2oc, k1sn, incsn. *(11 sts)*
Row 16: P1sn, p4oc, p6sn.
Row 17: Incsn, k4sn, k5oc, incoc. *(13 sts)*
Row 18: P7oc, p6sn.
Row 19: Cast (bind) off 6 sts sn, k7oc icos (hold 7 sts on spare needle for Right Side of Body).

Left Front Leg

Work as for Right Back Leg to *.
Work 7 rows st st.
Join in oc.
Row 15: Incsn, k1sn, k2oc, k4sn, incsn. *(11 sts)*
Row 16: P6sn, p4oc, p1sn.
Row 17: Incsn, k5oc, k4sn, incsn. *(13 sts)*
Row 18: P6sn, p7oc.
Row 19: K7oc, cast (bind) off 6 sts sn (hold 7 sts on spare needle for Left Side of Body).

Right Side of Body

Row 1: With oc and bl, cast on 1 st oc, with RS facing k7oc from spare needle of Right Front Leg, cast on 1 st oc and 5 sts bl. *(14 sts)*
Row 2: P5bl, p9oc.
Row 3: K9oc, k5bl, cast on 6 sts bl. *(20 sts)*
Row 4: P11bl, p9oc.
Join in sn.
Row 5: Incoc, k9oc, k10bl, cast on 2 sts bl and 2 sts oc, with RS facing k2oc, k3sn, k5oc from spare needle of Right Back Leg, cast on 1 st oc. *(36 sts)*

Row 6: P7oc, p2sn, p3oc, p13bl, p11oc.
Row 7: K11oc, k13bl, k3oc, k1sn, k8oc.
Row 8: P11oc, p14bl, p11oc.
Row 9: K11oc, k16bl, k9oc.
Row 10: P9oc, p15bl, p12oc.
Row 11: Incoc, k11oc, k16bl, k8oc. *(37 sts)*
Row 12: P7oc, p17bl, p12oc, p1sn.
Row 13: K1sn, k11oc, k19bl, k6oc.
Row 14: P5oc, p20bl, p10oc, p2sn.
Row 15: K2sn, k9oc, k23bl, k3oc.
Row 16: P2oc, p24bl, p6oc, p2bl, p3sn.
Row 17: K3sn, k3bl, k4oc, k27bl.
Row 18: P2togbl, p26bl, p2oc, p5bl, p2sn. *(36 sts)*
Row 19: K1sn, k33bl, k2togbl. *(35 sts)*
Row 20: P5bl (hold 5 sts on spare needle for tail), cast (bind) off 19 sts bl, p10bl icos, p1sn (hold 11 sts on spare needle for right neck).

Left Side of Body

Row 1: With oc and bl, cast on 1 st oc, with WS facing p7oc from spare needle of Left Front Leg, cast on 1 st oc and 5 sts bl. *(14 sts)*
Row 2: K5bl, k9oc.
Row 3: P9oc, p5bl, cast on 6 sts bl. *(20 sts)*
Row 4: K11bl, k9oc.
Join in sn.
Row 5: Incoc, p9oc, p10bl, cast on 2 sts bl and 2 sts oc, with WS facing p2oc, p3sn, p5oc from spare needle of Left Back Leg, cast on 1 st oc. *(36 sts)*
Row 6: K7oc, k2sn, k3oc, k13bl, k11oc.
Row 7: P11oc, p13bl, p3oc, p1sn, p8oc.
Row 8: K11oc, k14bl, k11oc.
Row 9: P11oc, p16bl, p9oc.
Row 10: K9oc, k15bl, k12oc.
Row 11: Incoc, p11oc, p16bl, p8oc. *(37 sts)*
Row 12: K7oc, k17bl, k12oc, k1sn.
Row 13: P1sn, p11oc, p19bl, p6oc.
Row 14: K5oc, k20bl, k10oc, k2sn.
Row 15: P2sn, p9oc, p23bl, p3oc.
Row 16: K2oc, k24bl, k6oc, k2bl, k3sn.
Row 17: P3sn, p3bl, p4oc, p27bl.

Row 18: K2togbl, k26bl, k2oc, k5bl, k2sn. *(36 sts)*
Row 19: P1sn, p33bl, p2togbl. *(35 sts)*
Row 20: K5bl (hold 5 sts on spare needle for tail), cast (bind) off 19 sts bl, k10bl icos, k1sn (hold 11 sts on spare needle for left neck).

Neck and Head

Row 1: With sn and bl, k2sn, k9bl held for neck from spare needle of Right Side of Body, then k9bl, k2sn held for neck from spare needle of Left Side of Body. *(22 sts)* Join in oc.
Row 2: P2sn, p2oc, p14bl, p2oc, p2sn.
Row 3: K2sn, k2oc, k2togoc, k10bl, k2togoc, k2oc, k2sn. *(20 sts)*
Row 4: P1sn, p6oc, p6bl, p6oc, p1sn.
Row 5: K1sn, k8oc, k2bl, k8oc, k1sn. Cont in oc.
Row 6: Purl.
Row 7: K17, wrap and turn (leave 3 sts on left-hand needle unworked).
Row 8: Working top of head on centre 14 sts only, p14, w&t.
Row 9: K14, w&t.
Rep rows 8–9 once more.
Row 12: P14, w&t.
Row 13: Knit across all sts. *(20 sts in total)*
Work 2 rows st st.
Row 16: P2tog, p16, p2tog. *(18 sts)*
Row 17: K15, w&t (leave 3 sts on left-hand needle unworked).
Join in sn.
Row 18: Working top of head on centre 12 sts only, p5oc, p2sn, p5oc, w&t.
Row 19: K5oc, k2sn, k5oc, w&t.
Rep rows 18–19 once more.
Row 22: P5oc, p2sn, p5oc, w&t.
Row 23: K4oc, k4sn, k7oc. *(18 sts in total)*
Row 24: P4oc, p2togoc, p2sn, p2togsn, p2sn, p2togoc, p4oc. *(15 sts)*
Row 25: K4oc, k2togsn, k3sn, k2togsn, k4oc. *(13 sts)*

Body
Use the intarsia technique and a separate ball of each colour yarn, twisting the colours firmly over one another at the joins to prevent holes forming.

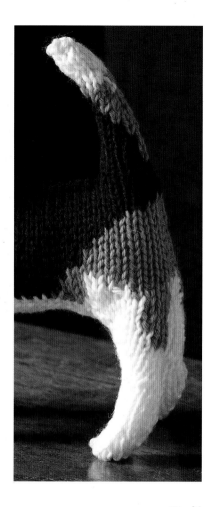

Row 26: P4oc, p5sn, p4oc.
Row 27: K3oc, k7sn, k3oc.
Row 28: P2oc, p9sn, p2oc.
Cont in sn.
Work 3 rows st st.
Row 32: P2tog, p9, p2tog. *(11 sts)*
Row 33: Knit.
Row 34: P2tog, p7, p2tog. *(9 sts)*
Cast (bind) off.

Tail

Row 1: With bl and with RS facing, k5 held for tail from spare needle of Left Side of Body, then k5 held for tail from spare needle of Right Side of Body. *(10 sts)*
Row 2: Purl.
Join in oc.
Row 3: K1oc, k8bl, k1oc.
Row 4: P1oc, p8bl, p1oc.
Rep rows 3–4 once more.
Row 7: K2oc, k6bl, k2oc.
Row 8: P2oc, p6bl, p2oc.
Row 9: K3oc, k4bl, k3oc.
Row 10: P3oc, p4bl, p3oc.
Row 11: K2togoc, k2oc, [incbl] twice, k2oc, k2togoc. *(10 sts)*
Row 12: P3oc, p4bl, p3oc.
Join in sn.
Row 13: K2togsn, k2oc, [incbl] twice, k2oc, k2togsn. *(10 sts)*
Row 14: P1sn, p3oc, p2bl, p3oc, p1sn.
Row 15: K3sn, k4oc, k3sn.
Row 16: P4sn, p2oc, p4sn.
Cont in sn.
Row 17: K2tog, k6, k2tog. *(8 sts)*
Work 3 rows st st.
Row 21: K2tog, k4, k2tog. *(6 sts)*
Row 22: P2tog, p2, p2tog. *(4 sts)*
Row 23: [K2tog] twice. *(2 sts)*
Row 24: P2tog and fasten off.

Tail

Use a pipecleaner to stiffen the upright tail.

Tummy

With sn, cast on 6 sts.
Beg with a k row, work 2 rows st st.
Row 3: K2tog, k2, k2tog. *(4 sts)*
Work 11 rows st st.
Row 15: Inc, k2, inc. *(6 sts)*
Work 7 rows st st.
Row 23: Inc, k4, inc. *(8 sts)*
Work 21 rows st st.
Row 45: K2tog, k4, k2tog. *(6 sts)*
Work 5 rows st st.
Row 51: Inc, k4, inc. *(8 sts)*
Work 9 rows st st.
Row 61: K2tog, k4, k2tog. *(6 sts)*
Work 17 rows st st.
Row 79: K2tog k2, k2tog. *(4 sts)*
Work 9 rows st st.
Cast (bind) off.

Ear

(make 2 the same)
With oc, cast on 4 sts.
Row 1: Inc, k2, inc. *(6 sts)*
Row 2: Knit.
Row 3: Inc, k4, inc. *(8 sts)*
Knit 10 rows.
Row 14: K2tog, k4, k2tog. *(6 sts)*
Knit 2 rows.
Row 17: K2tog, k2, k2tog. *(4 sts)*
Knit 2 rows.
Row 20: [K2tog] twice. *(2 sts)*
Cast (bind) off.

Collar

With bb, cast on 26 sts.
Knit one row.
Cast (bind) off.

To Make Up

See also diagram and notes on page 173.

SEWING IN ENDS Sew in ends, leaving ends from cast on and cast (bound) off rows for sewing up.

LEGS With WS together, fold leg in half. Starting at paw, sew up leg on RS.

BODY Sew along back of dog to tail.

TAIL Cut a pipecleaner 2.5cm (1in) longer than tail. Roll a little stuffing around pipecleaner, wrap tail around pipecleaner and sew up tail on RS, sewing down to bottom of bottom. Protruding end of pipecleaner will vanish into body stuffing.

HEAD Fold cast (bound) off row of head in half and sew from nose to chin.

TUMMY Sew cast on row of tummy to bottom of dog's bottom (where back legs begin), and sew cast (bound) off row to chin. Ease and sew tummy to fit body, matching curves of tummy to legs. Leave a 2.5cm (1in) gap between front and back legs on one side.

STUFFING Pipecleaners are used to stiffen the legs and help bend them into shape. Fold a pipecleaner into a 'U' shape and measure against front two legs. Cut to approximately fit, leaving an extra 2.5cm (1in) at both ends. Fold these ends over to stop pipecleaner poking out of paws. Roll a little stuffing around pipecleaner and slip into body, one end down each front leg. Repeat with second pipecleaner and back legs. Starting at the head, stuff the dog firmly, then sew up the gap. Mould body into shape.

EARS Sew cast on row of each ear to side of dog's head at an angle sloping down towards back, so 4 sts between front of ears, 10 sts between back of ears.

EYES With bl, sew 2-loop French knots positioned as in photograph.

NOSE With bl, embroider nose in satin stitch.

COLLAR Sew ends of collar together and pop over head.

Bernese Mountain Dog

A beautiful, sturdy dog from Switzerland, the Bernese Mountain Dog is a traditional working farm dog. A gentle giant, they are more than happy to play with children and be hitched up to a small cart – an alternative nanny? Unfortunately they are prone to mobility problems and are susceptible to cancer, which can shorten their life span. Robert Pattinson of *Twilight* fame is a proud Bernese Mountain Dog owner.

Bernese Mountain Dog

The Bernese Mountain Dog is very rewarding to make; you can always alter the markings to match your dog.

Measurements

Length: 18cm (7in)
Height to top of head: 18cm (7in)

Materials

- Pair of 2¾mm (US 2) knitting needles
- Double-pointed 2¾mm (US 2) knitting needles (for holding stitches and for tail)
- 10g (¼oz) of Rowan Creative Focus Worsted in Natural 00100 (na)
- 5g (⅙oz) of Rowan Creative Focus Worsted in Golden Heather 00018 (gh)
- 15g (½oz) of Rowan Creative Focus Worsted in Ebony 00500 (eb)
- 2 pipecleaners for legs

Abbreviations

See page 172.
See page 172 for Colour Knitting.
See page 172 for I-cord Technique.
See page 172 for Wrap and Turn Method.
See page 172 for Loopy Stitch. Work 2-finger loopy stitch throughout this pattern.

Right Back Leg

With na, cast on 11 sts.
Beg with a k row, work 2 rows st st.
Cont in gh.

Row 3: Inc, k2, k2tog, k1, k2tog, k2, inc. *(11 sts)*
Row 4: Purl.
Rep rows 3–4 once more.*
Join in eb.
Row 7: K9gh, k2eb.
Row 8: P2eb, p9gh.
Row 9: K8gh, k3eb.
Row 10: P3eb, p8gh.
Row 11: K2toggh, k2gh, incgh, k1gh, incgh, k2eb, k2togeb. *(11 sts)*
Row 12: P3eb, p8gh.
Row 13: K2toggh, k2gh, incgh, k1gh, incgh, k2eb, k2togeb. *(11 sts)*
Row 14: P4eb, p7gh.
Row 15: K4gh, incgh, k1gh, incgh, k4eb. *(13 sts)*
Row 16: P5eb, p8gh.
Row 17: K5gh, incgh, k1eb, inceb, k5eb. *(15 sts)*
Row 18: P6eb, inceb, p1eb, incgh, p6gh. *(17 sts)*
Row 19: K7gh, incgh, k1eb, inceb, k7eb. *(19 sts)*
Row 20: P8eb, inceb, p1eb, incgh, p8gh. *(21 sts)*
Row 21: K9gh, incgh, k1eb, inceb, k9eb. *(23 sts)*
Row 22: P12eb, p11gh.
Row 23: Cast (bind) off 11 sts gh, k12eb icos (hold 12 sts on spare needle for Right Side of Body).

Left Back Leg

Work as for Right Back Leg to *.
Join in eb.
Row 7: K2eb, k9gh.
Row 8: P9gh, p2eb.
Row 9: K3eb, k8gh.
Row 10: P8gh, p3eb.
Row 11: K2togeb, k2eb, incgh, k1gh, incgh, k2gh, k2toggh. *(11 sts)*
Row 12: P8gh, p3eb.
Row 13: K2togeb, k2eb, incgh, k1gh, incgh, k2gh, k2toggh. *(11 sts)*

Row 14: P7gh, p4eb.
Row 15: K4eb, incgh, k1gh, incgh, k4gh. *(13 sts)*
Row 16: P8gh, p5eb.
Row 17: K5eb, inceb, k1eb, incgh, k5gh. *(15 sts)*
Row 18: P6gh, incgh, p1eb, inceb, p6eb. *(17 sts)*
Row 19: K7eb, inceb, k1eb, incgh, k7gh. *(19 sts)*
Row 20: P8gh, incgh, p1eb, inceb, p8eb. *(21 sts)*
Row 21: K9eb, inceb, k1eb, incgh, k9gh. *(23 sts)*
Row 22: P11gh, p12eb.
Row 23: K12eb, cast (bind) off 11 sts gh (hold 12 sts on spare needle for Left Side of Body).

Right Front Leg

Work as for Right Back Leg to *.
Work 4 rows st st.
Join in eb.
Row 11: K4gh, k2eb, k3gh, k2eb.
Row 12: P3eb, p2gh, p2eb, p4gh.
Row 13: Incgh, k2gh, k7eb, inceb. *(13 sts)*
Cont in eb.
Work 3 rows st st.
Row 17: Inc, k11, inc. *(15 sts)*
Row 18: Purl.
Row 19: Cast (bind) off 7 sts, k to end (hold 8 sts on spare needle for Right Side of Body).

Left Front Leg

Work as for Right Back Leg to *.
Work 4 rows st st.
Join in eb.
Row 11: K2eb, k3gh, k2eb, k4gh.
Row 12: P4gh, p2eb, p2gh, p3eb.
Row 13: Inceb, k7eb, k2gh, incgh. *(13 sts)*
Cont in eb.
Work 3 rows st st.
Row 17: Inc, k11, inc. *(15 sts)*
Row 18: Purl.
Row 19: K8, cast (bind) off 7 sts (hold 8 sts on spare needle for Left Side of Body).

Right Side of Body

Row 1: With eb, cast on 1 st, with RS facing k8 from spare needle of Right Front Leg, cast on 5 sts. *(14 sts)*
Row 2: Purl.
Row 3: Inc, k7, loopy st 5, k1, cast on 4 sts. *(19 sts)*
Row 4: Purl.
Row 5: K14, loopy st 4, k1, cast on 3 sts, with RS facing k12 from spare needle of Right Back Leg, cast on 2 sts. *(36 sts)*
Row 6: Purl.
Row 7: Inc, k17, loopy st 3, k15. *(37 sts)*
Work 3 rows st st.
Row 11: Inc, k36. *(38 sts)*
Work 3 rows st st.
Join in na.
Row 15: K1na, k37eb.
Row 16: P36eb, p2na.
Row 17: K2na, k36eb.
Row 18: P2togeb, p33eb, p3na. *(37 sts)*
Row 19: K3na, k32eb, k2togeb. *(36 sts)*
Row 20: P2togeb, p30eb, p4na. *(35 sts)*
Row 21: K4na, k29eb, k2togeb. *(34 sts)*
Row 22: Cast (bind) off 23 sts eb, p7eb icos, p4na (hold 11 sts on spare needle for right neck).

Left Side of Body

Row 1: With eb, cast on 1 st, with WS facing p8 from spare needle of Left Front Leg, cast on 5 sts. *(14 sts)*
Row 2: Knit.
Row 3: Inc, p13, cast on 4 sts. *(19 sts)*
Row 4: K4, loopy st 5, k10.
Row 5: P19, cast on 3 sts, with WS facing p12 from spare needle of Left Back Leg, cast on 2 sts. *(36 sts)*
Row 6: K17, loopy st 4, k15.
Row 7: Inc, p35. *(37 sts)*
Row 8: K14, loopy st 3, k20.
Work 2 rows st st.
Row 11: Inc, p36. *(38 sts)*
Work 3 rows st st.
Join in na.

Row 15: P1na, p37eb.
Row 16: K36eb, k2na.
Row 17: P2na, p36eb.
Row 18: K2togeb, k33eb, k3na. *(37 sts)*
Row 19: P3na, p32eb, p2togeb. *(36 sts)*
Row 20: K2togeb, k30eb, k4na. *(35 sts)*
Row 21: P4na, p29eb, p2togeb. *(34 sts)*
Row 22: Cast (bind) off 23 sts eb, k7eb icos, k4na (hold 11 sts on spare needle for left neck).

Neck and Head

Row 1: With na and eb and with RS facing, k4na, k7eb held for neck from spare needle of Right Side of Body, then k7eb, k4na held for neck from spare needle of Left Side of Body. *(22 sts)*
Row 2: P3na, p16eb, p3na.
Row 3: K2na, k3eb, k2togeb, k8eb, k2togeb, k3eb, k2na. *(20 sts)*
Row 4: P1na, p18eb, p1na.
Cont in eb.
Row 5: Inc, k18, inc. *(22 sts)*
Row 6: Purl.
Row 7: Inc, k4, k2tog, k8, k2tog, k4, inc. *(22 sts)*
Row 8: Purl.
Row 9: K18, wrap and turn (leave 4 sts on left-hand needle unworked).
Row 10: Working top of head on centre 14 sts only, p14, w&t.
Row 11: K14, w&t.
Rep rows 10–11 once more.
Row 14: P14, w&t.
Row 15: Knit across all sts. *(22 sts in total)*
Join in na.
Row 16: P10eb, p2na, p10eb.
Row 17: K10eb, k2na, k10eb.
Row 18: P10eb, p2na, p10eb.
Join in gh.
Row 19: K1gh, k9eb, k2na, k6eb, w&t (leave 4 sts on left-hand needle unworked).
Row 20: Working top of head on centre 14 sts only, p6eb, p2na, p6eb, w&t.

Legs

The Bernese Mountain Dog has large paws, so use a knitting needle to push stuffing down into them.

Row 21: K6eb, k2na, k6eb, w&t.
Rep rows 20–21 once more.
Row 24: P6eb, p2na, p6eb, w&t.
Join in another strand of gh.
Row 25: K3eb, k1gh, k1eb, k4na, k1eb, k1gh, k6eb, k1gh. *(22 sts in total)*
Row 26: P2gh, p2togeb, p2eb, p2togeb, p1gh, p4na, p1gh, p2togeb, p2eb, p2togeb, p2gh. *(18 sts)*
Row 27: K4gh, k1eb, k2togna, k4na, k2togna, k1eb, k4gh. *(16 sts)*
Row 28: P5gh, p6na, p5gh.
Cont in na.
Row 29: K2tog, k2, k2tog, k4, k2tog, k2, k2tog. *(12 sts)*
Work 4 rows st st.
Row 34: P2tog, p8, p2tog. *(10 sts)*
Row 35: Knit.
Cast (bind) off 10 sts.

Tail

With two double-pointed needles and na, cast on 2 sts.
Work in i-cord as folls:
Row 1: Knit.
Row 2: [Inc] twice. *(4 sts)*
Row 3: Knit.
Row 4: Inc, k2, inc. *(6 sts)*
Row 5: Knit.
Cont in eb.
Knit 2 rows.
Row 8: Inc, k4, inc. *(8 sts)*
Knit 2 rows.
Row 11: K1, loopy st 1, k4, loopy st 1, k1.
Knit 3 rows.
Rep last 4 rows 4 times more.
Knit 4 rows.
Cast (bind) off.

Tummy

With eb, cast on 6 sts.
Beg with a k row, work 4 rows st st.
Join in na.
Row 5: K2eb, k2na, k2eb.
Row 6: P2eb, p2na, p2eb.
Row 7: K1eb, k4na, k1eb.
Row 8: P1eb, p4na, p1eb.
Cont in na.
Work 12 rows st st.
Row 21: Inc, k4, inc. *(8 sts)*
Work 19 rows st st.
Row 41: K2tog, k4, k2tog. *(6 sts)*
Work 4 rows st st.
Row 46: Inc, p4, inc. *(8 sts)*
Work 8 rows st st.
Row 55: K1, loopy st 1, k4, loopy st 1, k1.
Work 3 rows st st.
Rep last 4 rows 5 times more.
Work 2 rows st st.
Row 81: K2tog, k4, k2tog. *(6 sts)*
Work 7 rows st st.
Row 89: K2tog, k2, k2tog. *(4 sts)*
Work 6 rows st st.
Cast (bind) off.

Ear

(make 2 the same)
With eb, cast on 7 sts.
Knit 10 rows.
Row 11: K2tog, k5. *(6 sts)*
Row 12: Knit.
Row 13: K2tog, k4. *(5 sts)*
Row 14: Knit.
Row 15: K2tog, k1, k2tog. *(3 sts)*
Row 16: Knit.
Cast (bind) off 3 sts.

Tail

You can use a pipecleaner to stuff the tail if you want to.

To Make Up

See also diagram and notes on page 173.

SEWING IN ENDS Sew in ends, leaving ends from cast on and cast (bound) off rows for sewing up.

LEGS With WS together, fold leg in half. Starting at paw, sew up leg on RS.

BODY Sew along back of dog and around bottom.

HEAD Fold cast (bound) off row of head in half and sew from nose to chin.

TUMMY Sew cast on row of tummy to top of dog's bottom (where back legs begin), and sew cast (bound) off row to chin. Ease and sew tummy to fit body. Leave a 2.5cm (1in) gap between front and back legs on one side.

STUFFING Pipecleaners are used to stiffen the legs and help bend them into shape. Fold a pipecleaner into a 'U' shape and measure against front two legs. Cut to approximately fit, leaving an extra 2.5cm (1in) at both ends. Fold these ends over to stop pipecleaner poking out of paws. Roll a little stuffing around pipecleaner and slip into body, one end down each front leg. Repeat with second pipecleaner and back legs. Starting at the head, stuff the dog firmly, then sew up the gap. Mould body into shape.

TAIL Sew cast (bound) off end of tail to dog where back meets bottom. The tail will naturally curl, but for more of a bend slip a pipecleaner in to it.

EARS Sew cast on row of each ear to side of dog's head, following natural slope of head and with 6 sts between ears. Catch tip of ears down with a stitch.

EYES With eb, sew 3-loop French knots positioned as in photograph.

NOSE With eb, embroider nose in satin stitch.

Boxer

The Boxer, now in the top ten of popular dogs, was originally developed in Germany in the 19th century, a cross between something called a Brabantian Bullenbeiser and an English Bulldog. Bengo, the cartoon Boxer, and his friends Simon and Mitzi were very much a feature of a 1950s childhood. Tail docking has been banned since 2007, but ours is a pre-2007 Boxer; if you want to have an undocked tail you can make it longer.

Boxer

The Boxer is a fairly simple and quick dog to knit.

Measurements

Length: 19cm (7½in)
Height to top of head: 17cm (6¾in)

Materials

- Pair of 2¾mm (US 2) knitting needles
- Double-pointed 2¾mm (US 2) knitting needles (for holding stitches)
- 15g (½oz) of Rowan Creative Focus Worsted in Natural 00100 (na)
- 25g (1oz) of Rowan Creative Focus Worsted in Golden Heather 00018 (gh)
- Small amount of Rowan Pure Wool 4ply in Eau de Nil 450 (en) for collar
- 2 pipecleaners for legs
- Tiny amount of Rowan Pure Wool 4ply in Black 404 (bl) for eyes and nose

Abbreviations

See page 172.
See page 172 for Colour Knitting.
See page 172 for Wrap and Turn Method.

Right Back Leg

With na, cast on 7 sts.
Beg with a k row, work 2 rows st st.
Row 3: Inc, k2tog, k1, k2tog, inc. *(7 sts)*
Work 3 rows st st.
Cont in gh.
Work 6 rows st st.
Row 13: K2tog, inc, k1, inc, k2tog. *(7 sts)*
Row 14 and every alt row: Purl.
Row 15: K2tog, inc, k1, inc, k2tog. *(7 sts)*
Row 17: K2tog, [inc] 3 times, k2tog. *(8 sts)*
Row 19: K1, [inc] 6 times, k1. *(14 sts)*
Row 21: K2tog, [inc] 3 times, k4, [inc] 3 times, k2tog. *(18 sts)*
Row 23: Knit.
Row 25: K2tog, [inc] twice, k10, [inc] twice, k2tog.* *(20 sts)*
Row 27: Cast (bind) off 10 sts, k to end (hold 10 sts on spare needle for Right Side of Body).

Left Back Leg

Work as for Right Back Leg to *.
Row 26: Purl.
Row 27: K10, cast (bind) off 10 sts (hold 10 sts on spare needle for Left Side of Body).

Right Front Leg

With na, cast on 7 sts.
Beg with a k row, work 2 rows st st.
Row 3: Inc, k2tog, k1, k2tog, inc. *(7 sts)*
Row 4: Purl.
Work 2 rows st st.
Row 7: Inc, k5, inc. *(9 sts)*
Work 3 rows st st.
Join in gh.
Row 11: K5na, k4gh.
Cont in gh.
Work 7 rows st st.
Row 19: Inc, k7, inc. *(11 sts)*
Row 20: Purl.**
Row 21: Cast (bind) off 5 sts, k to end (hold 6 sts on spare needle for Right Side of Body).

Body

The Boxer has a shapely waist.

Left Front Leg

Work as for Right Front Leg to **.
Row 21: K6, cast (bind) off 5 sts (hold 6 sts on spare needle for Left Side of Body).

Right Side of Body

Row 1: With gh, cast on 1 st, with RS facing k6 from spare needle of Right Front Leg, cast on 3 sts. *(10 sts)*
Row 2: Purl.
Row 3: K10, cast on 4 sts. *(14 sts)*
Row 4: Purl.
Row 5: Inc, k13, cast on 3 sts. *(18 sts)*
Row 6: Purl.
Row 7: K18, cast on 4 sts. *(22 sts)*
Row 8: Purl.
Row 9: Inc, k21, with RS facing k10 from spare needle of Right Back Leg. *(33 sts)*
Work 7 rows st st.
Row 17: K31, k2tog. *(32 sts)*
Row 18: Purl.
Row 19: Inc, k29, k2tog. *(32 sts)*
Row 20: P2tog, p30. *(31 sts)*
Row 21: K29, k2tog. *(30 sts)*
Row 22: Cast (bind) off 20 sts, p to end (hold 10 sts on spare needle for right neck).

Left Side of Body

Row 1: With gh, cast on 1 st, with WS facing p6 from spare needle of Left Front Leg, cast on 3 sts. *(10 sts)*
Row 2: Knit.
Row 3: P10, cast on 4 sts. *(14 sts)*
Row 4: Knit.
Row 5: Inc, p13, cast on 3 sts. *(18 sts)*
Row 6: Knit.
Row 7: P18, cast on 4 sts. *(22 sts)*
Row 8: Knit.
Row 9: Inc, p21, with WS facing p10 from spare needle of Left Back Leg. *(33 sts)*
Work 7 rows st st.
Row 17: P31, p2tog. *(32 sts)*
Row 18: Knit.
Row 19: Inc, p29, p2tog. *(32 sts)*
Row 20: K2tog, k30. *(31 sts)*
Row 21: P29, p2tog. *(30 sts)*
Row 22: Cast (bind) off 20 sts, k to end (hold 10 sts on spare needle for left neck).

Head

The Boxer's head is sewn up in a similar way to all the dogs, but the nose is folded back on itself to create the snub face.

Neck and Head

Row 1: With gh and with RS facing, k10 held for neck from spare needle of Right Side of Body, then k10 held for neck from spare needle of Left Side of Body. *(20 sts)*
Row 2: P1, p2tog, p14, p2tog, p1. *(18 sts)*
Row 3: K1, k2tog, k12, k2tog, k1. *(16 sts)*
Row 4: Purl.
Row 5: K7, k2tog, k7. *(15 sts)*
Row 6: P1, inc, p1, inc, p7, inc, p1, inc, p1. *(19 sts)*
Row 7: K17, wrap and turn (leave 2 sts on left-hand needle unworked).
Row 8: Working top of head on centre 15 sts only, p15, w&t.
Row 9: K15, w&t.
Row 10: P15, w&t.
Row 11: K15, w&t.
Row 12: P15, w&t.
Row 13: Knit across all sts. *(19 sts in total)*
Row 14: Purl.
Join in na.
Row 15: K9gh, k1na, k9gh.
Row 16: P9gh, p1na, p9gh.
Row 17: K9gh, k1na, k6gh, w&t (leave 3 sts on left-hand needle unworked).
Row 18: Working top of head on centre 13 sts only, p6gh, p1na, p6gh, w&t.
Row 19: K6gh, k1na, k6gh, w&t.
Row 20: P6gh, p1na, p6gh, w&t.
Row 21: K6gh, k1na, k9gh. *(19 sts in total)*
Row 22: P5gh, [p2toggh] twice, p1na, [p2toggh] twice, p5gh. *(15 sts)*
Row 23: K4gh, k1na, k2togna, k1na, k2togna, k1na, k4gh. *(13 sts)*
Row 24: Incgh, p1gh, p2togna, p5na, p2togna, p1gh, incgh. *(13 sts)*
Cont in na.
Row 25: K1, [inc] twice, k1, k2tog, k1, k2tog, k1, [inc] twice, k1. *(15 sts)*
Work 3 rows st st.

Row 27: K2tog, k11, k2tog. *(13 sts)*
Row 28: Cast (bind) off 5 sts, p3 icos, cast (bind) off 5 sts.
Rejoin na to rem sts.
Row 29: K3tog and fasten off.

Tail

With gh, cast on 5 sts.
Beg with a k row, work 5 rows st st.
Cast (bind) off.

Tummy

With gh, cast on 1 st.
Row 1: Inc. *(2 sts)*
Row 2: [Inc] twice. *(4 sts)*
Row 3: Inc, p2, inc. *(6 sts)*
Row 4: Inc, k4, inc. *(8 sts)*
Work 11 rows st st.
Join in na.
Row 16: K2gh, k4na, k2gh.
Row 17: P1gh, p6na, p1gh.
Cont in na.
Work 44 rows st st.
Row 62: K2tog, k4, k2tog. *(6 sts)*
Work 15 rows st st.
Row 78: K2tog, k2, k2tog. *(4 sts)*
Work 13 rows st st.
Cast (bind) off.

Ear

(make 2 the same)
With gh, cast on 7 sts.
Beg with a k row, work 5 rows st st.
Row 6: P2tog, p3, p2tog. *(5 sts)*
Row 7: K2tog, k1, k2tog. *(3 sts)*
Row 8: Purl.
Row 9: K3tog and fasten off.

Collar

With en, cast on 28 sts.
Knit one row.
Cast (bind) off.

To Make Up

See also diagram and notes on page 173.

SEWING IN ENDS Sew in ends, leaving ends from cast on and cast (bound) off rows for sewing up.

LEGS With WS together, fold leg in half. Starting at paw, sew up leg on RS.

BODY Sew along back of dog and around bottom.

HEAD Fold cast (bound) off row of head in half and sew 1cm (⅜in) down nose. Fold final row of nose back on itself and sew down with 2 horizontal satin sts to approx row 21 of head.

TUMMY Sew cast on row of tummy to twhere you have finished sewing down bottom, and sew cast (bound) off row to chin. Ease and sew tummy to fit body. Leave a 2.5cm (1in) gap between front and back legs on one side.

STUFFING Pipecleaners are used to stiffen the legs and help bend them into shape. Fold a pipecleaner into a 'U' shape and measure against front two legs. Cut to approximately fit, leaving an extra 2.5cm (1in) at both ends. Fold these ends over to stop pipecleaner poking out of paws. Roll a little stuffing around pipecleaner and slip into body, one end down each front leg. Repeat with second pipecleaner and back legs. Starting at the head, stuff the dog firmly, then sew up the gap. Mould body into shape.

TAIL Sew up tail on RS and sew to dog where back meets bottom.

EARS Sew cast on row of each ear to side of dog's head, following natural slope of head and with 3 sts between ears.

EYES With bl, sew 3-loop French knots positioned as in photograph.

NOSE With bl, embroider nose in satin stitch.

COLLAR Sew ends of collar together and pop over head.

Doberman Pinscher

Fiercely loyal, this magnificent dog will protect and defend its owners and their property. The Doberman's past reputation has been for aggression, but this has now changed and they are considered to be wonderful and intelligent family dogs. Hunter S. Thompson owned several Dobermans and trained his dog, Bronco, to attack on the command word 'Nixon'. Chef Jean Christophe Novelli owns an entire pack of Dobermans, twenty-one of them apparently.

Doberman Pinscher

Ours is a hunting Doberman, for an undocked tail, follow the Weimaraner tail instructions (page 116).

Measurements

Length: 19cm (7½in)
Height to top of head: 18cm (7in)

Materials

- Pair of 2¾mm (US 2) knitting needles
- Double-pointed 2¾mm (US 2) knitting needles (for holding stitches)
- 10g (¼oz) of Rowan Pure Wool 4ply in Ochre 461 (oc)
- 15g (½oz) of Rowan Cashsoft 4ply in Black 422 (bl)
- Small amount of Rowan Cashsoft 4ply in Quartz 446 (qu) for collar
- 2 pipecleaners for legs
- 2 tiny black beads for eyes and sewing needle and black thread for sewing on

Abbreviations

See page 172.
See page 172 for Colour Knitting.
See page 172 for Wrap and Turn Method.

Right Back Leg

With oc, cast on 11 sts.
Beg with a k row, work 2 rows st st.
Row 3: Inc, k2, k2tog, k1, k2tog, k2, inc. *(11 sts)*
Row 4: Purl
Rep rows 3–4 once more.
Row 7: K2tog, k1, k2tog, k1, k2tog, k1, k2tog.* *(7 sts)*
Work 3 rows st st.
Join in bl.
Row 11: K1bl, k5oc, k1bl.
Row 12: P1bl, p5oc, p1bl.
Row 13: K2togbl, incoc, k1oc, incoc, k2togbl. *(7 sts)*
Row 14: P2bl, incoc, p1oc, incoc, p2bl. *(9 sts)*
Row 15: K2togbl, k1bl, incoc, k1oc, incoc, k1bl, k2togbl. *(9 sts)*
Row 16: P2bl, p5oc, p2bl.**
Row 17: K2bl, k1oc, incoc, k1oc, incoc, k3bl. *(11 sts)*
Row 18: P3bl, p6oc, p2bl.
Row 19: K2bl, k2oc, incoc, k1oc, incoc, k4bl. *(13 sts)*
Row 20: P4bl, p7oc, p2bl.
Row 21: K2bl, k3oc, incoc, k1oc, incoc, k5bl. *(15 sts)*
Row 22: P6bl, p7oc, p2bl.
Row 23: K2bl, k4oc, incoc, k1oc, incbl, k6bl. *(17 sts)*
Row 24: P8bl, p7oc, p2bl.
Row 25: K2bl, k7oc, k8bl.
Row 26: P8bl, p7oc, p2bl.
Row 27: K2bl, k5oc, incoc, k1bl, incbl, k7bl. *(19 sts)*
Row 28: P10bl, p7oc, p2bl.
Row 29: K2bl, k6oc, incoc, k1bl, incbl, k8bl. *(21 sts)*
Row 30: P11bl, p8oc, p2bl.
Row 31: Cast (bind) off 2 sts bl and 8 sts oc, k11bl icos (hold 11 sts on spare needle for Right Side of Body).

Left Back Leg

Work as for Right Back Leg to **.
Row 17: K3bl, incoc, k1oc, incoc, k1oc, k2bl. *(11 sts)*
Row 18: P2bl, p6oc, p3bl.
Row 19: K4bl, incoc, k1oc, incoc, k2oc, k2bl. *(13 sts)*
Row 20: P2bl, p7oc, p4bl.
Row 21: K5bl, incoc, k1oc, incoc, k3oc, k2bl. *(15 sts)*
Row 22: P2bl, p7oc, p6bl.
Row 23: K6bl, incbl, k1oc, incoc, k4oc, k2bl. *(17 sts)*
Row 24: P2bl, p7oc, p8bl.
Row 25: K8bl, k7oc, k2bl.
Row 26: P2bl, p7oc, p8bl.
Row 27: K7bl, incbl, k1bl, incoc, k5oc, k2bl. *(19 sts)*
Row 28: P2bl, p7oc, p10bl.
Row 29: K8bl, incbl, k1bl, incoc, k6oc, k2bl. *(21 sts)*
Row 30: P2bl, p8oc, p11bl.
Row 31: K11bl, cast (bind) off 2 sts bl and 8 sts oc (hold 11 sts on spare needle for Left Side of Body).

Right Front Leg

Work as for Right Back Leg to *.
Work 5 rows st st.***
Join in bl.
Row 13: K4oc, k1bl, k2oc.
Row 14: P2oc, p2bl, p3oc.
Row 15: Incoc, k2oc, k2bl, k1oc, incoc. *(9 sts)*
Row 16: P3oc, p2bl, p4oc.
Row 17: K4oc, k3bl, k2oc.
Row 18: P2oc, p3bl, p4oc.
Row 19: K3oc, k5bl, k1oc.
Row 20: P6bl, p3oc.
Row 21: Incoc, k1oc, k6bl, incbl. *(11 sts)*
Row 22: P9bl, p2oc.
Row 23: K1oc, k10bl.
Cont in bl.
Work 3 rows st st.
Row 27: Cast (bind) off 5 sts, k to end (hold 6 sts on spare needle for Right Side of Body).

Legs

Use pipecleaners and firmly stuff the front legs as Dobermans stand up very straight.

Left Front Leg

Work as for Right Front Leg to ***.

Join in bl.

Row 13: K2oc, k1bl, k4oc.

Row 14: P3oc, p2bl, p2oc.

Row 15: Incoc, k1oc, k2bl, k2oc, incoc. *(9 sts)*

Row 16: P4oc, p2bl, p3oc.

Row 17: K2oc, k3bl, k4oc.

Row 18: P4oc, p3bl, p2oc.

Row 19: K1oc, k5bl, k3oc.

Row 20: P3oc, p6bl.

Row 21: Incbl, k6bl, k1oc, incoc. *(11 sts)*

Row 22: P2oc, p9bl.

Row 23: K10bl, k1oc.

Cont in bl.

Work 3 rows st st.

Row 27: K6, cast (bind) off 5 sts (hold 6 sts on spare needle for Left Side of Body).

Right Side of Body

Row 1: With bl, cast on 1 st, with RS facing k6 from spare needle of Right Front Leg, cast on 6 sts. *(13 sts)*

Row 2: Purl.

Row 3: Inc, k12, cast on 4 sts. *(18 sts)*

Join in oc.

Row 4: P17bl, p1oc.

Row 5: Incoc, k17bl, cast on 3 sts bl. *(22 sts)*

Row 6: P20bl, p2oc.

Row 7: Incoc, k1oc, k20bl, cast on 4 sts bl. *(27 sts)*

Row 8: P24bl, p3oc.

Row 9: K3oc, k24bl, with RS facing k11bl from spare needle of Right Back Leg, cast on 2 sts bl. *(40 sts)*

Row 10: P38bl, p2oc.

Cont in bl.

Work 7 rows st st.

Row 18: P2tog, p38. *(39 sts)*

Row 19: K2tog, k37. *(38 sts)*

Row 20: Cast (bind) off 28 sts, p to end (hold 10 sts on spare needle for right neck).

Left Side of Body

Row 1: With bl, cast on 1 st, with WS facing p6 from spare needle of Left Front Leg, cast on 6 sts. *(13 sts)*

Row 2: Knit.

Row 3: Inc, p12, cast on 4 sts. *(18 sts)*

Join in oc.

Row 4: K17bl, k1oc.

Row 5: Incoc, p17bl, cast on 3 sts bl. *(22 sts)*

Row 6: K20bl, k2oc.

Row 7: Incoc, p1oc, p20bl, cast on 4 sts bl. *(27 sts)*

Row 8: K24bl, k3oc.

Row 9: P3oc, p24bl, with WS facing p11bl from spare needle of Left Back Leg, cast on 2 sts bl. *(40 sts)*

Row 10: K38bl, k2oc.

Cont in bl.

Work 7 rows st st.

Row 18: K2tog, k38. *(39 sts)*

Row 19: P2tog, p37. *(38 sts)*

Row 20: Cast (bind) off 28 sts, k to end (hold 10 sts on spare needle for left neck).

Neck and Head

Row 1: With bl and with RS facing, k10 held for neck from spare needle of Right Side of Body, then k10 held for neck from spare needle of Left Side of Body. *(20 sts)*

Row 2: Purl.

Row 3: K5, k2tog, k6, k2tog, k5. *(18 sts)*

Row 4: Purl.

Row 5: K5, k2tog, k4, k2tog, k5. *(16 sts)*

Row 6: Purl.

Row 7: K5, k2tog, k2, k2tog, k5. *(14 sts)*

Row 8: Purl.

Row 9: Inc, k11, wrap and turn (leave 2 sts on left-hand needle unworked).

Row 10: Working top of head on centre 10 sts only, p10, w&t.

Row 11: K10, w&t.

Rep rows 10–11 once more.

Row 14: P10, w&t.

Row 15: K11, inc. *(16 sts in total)*

Work 2 rows st st.
Row 18: P2tog, p12, p2tog. *(14 sts)*
Row 19: K12, w&t (leave 2 sts on left-hand needle unworked).
Row 20: P10, w&t.
Row 21: K10, w&t.
Rep rows 20–21 once more.
Row 24: P10, w&t.
Row 25: Knit across all sts. *(14 sts in total)*
Join in oc.
Row 26: P2oc, p2togbl, p2bl, p2togbl, p2bl, p2togbl, p2oc. *(11 sts)*
Row 27: K2oc, k2togoc, k3bl, k2togoc, k2oc. *(9 sts)*
Row 28: P2oc, p5bl, p2oc.
Row 29: K3oc, k3bl, k3oc.
Row 30: P3oc, p3bl, p3oc.
Row 31: K2oc, k2togbl, k1bl, k2togbl, k2oc. *(7 sts)*
Row 32: P2oc, p3bl, p2oc.
Row 33: K2oc, k3bl, k2oc.
Row 34: P2togoc, p3bl, p2togoc. *(5 sts)*
Cast (bind) off.

Tail

With bl, cast on 6 sts.
Beg with a k row, work 6 rows st st.
Cast (bind) off.

Tummy

With bl, cast on 6 sts.
Beg with a k row, work 2 rows st st.
Row 3: K2tog, k2, k2tog. *(4 sts)*
Work 13 rows st st.
Row 17: Inc, k2, inc. *(6 sts)*
Work 19 rows st st.
Row 37: K1, inc, k2, inc, k1. *(8 sts)*
Work 7 rows st st.
Row 45: K2tog, k4, k2tog. *(6 sts)*
Row 46: P2tog, p2, p2tog. *(4 sts)*
Work 2 rows st st.
Row 49: Inc, k2, inc. *(6 sts)*
Row 50: Inc, p4, inc. *(8 sts)*
Work 2 rows st st.
Join in oc.

Row 53: K1oc, k6bl, k1oc.
Row 54: P2oc, p4bl, p2oc.
Row 55: K2oc, k4bl, k2oc.
Row 56: P3oc, p2bl, p3oc.
Row 57: K3oc, k2bl, k3oc.
Row 58: P2oc, p4bl, p2oc.
Row 59: K2oc, k4bl, k2oc.
Cont in bl.
Work 13 rows st st.
Row 73: K2tog, k4, k2tog. *(6 sts)*
Work 7 rows st st.
Join in oc.
Row 81: K2bl, k2oc, k2bl.
Row 82: P2bl, p2oc, p2bl.
Rep rows 81–82 once more.
Row 85: K1bl, [k2togoc] twice, k1bl. *(4 sts)*
Row 86: P1bl, p2oc, p1bl.
Cont in oc.
Work 8 rows st st.
Row 95: [K2tog] twice. *(2 sts)*
Row 96: P2tog and fasten off.

Ear

(make 2 the same)
With bl, cast on 6 sts.
Knit 6 rows.
Row 7: K2tog, k2, k2tog. *(4 sts)*
Knit 4 rows.
Row 12: [K2tog] twice. *(2 sts)*
Knit 2 rows.
Row 15: K2tog and fasten off.

Collar

With qu, cast on 24 sts.
Knit one row.
Cast (bind) off.

Ears

Tweak the ears between finger and thumb so they are upright and perky to give added personality.

To Make Up

See also diagram and notes on page 173.

SEWING IN ENDS Sew in ends, leaving ends from cast on and cast (bound) off rows for sewing up.

LEGS With WS together, fold leg in half. Starting at paw, sew up leg on RS.

BODY Sew along back of dog and around bottom.

HEAD Fold cast (bound) off row of head in half and sew from nose to chin.

TUMMY Sew cast on row of tummy to bottom of dog's bottom (where back legs begin), and sew cast (bound) off row to chin. Ease and sew tummy to fit body, matching curves of tummy to legs. Leave a 2.5cm (1in) gap between front and back legs on one side.

STUFFING Pipecleaners are used to stiffen the legs and help bend them into shape. Fold a pipecleaner into a 'U' shape and measure against front two legs. Cut to approximately fit, leaving an extra 2.5cm (1in) at both ends. Fold these ends over to stop pipecleaner poking out of paws. Roll a little stuffing around pipecleaner and slip into body, one end down each front leg. Repeat with second pipecleaner and back legs. Starting at the head, stuff the dog firmly, then sew up the gap. Mould body into shape.

TAIL Sew up tail on RS and sew to dog where back meets bottom.

EARS Sew cast on row of each ear to side of dog's head, at a slight angle and with 3 sts between ears.

EYES Sew on black beads, positioned as in photograph.

NOSE With bl, embroider nose in satin stitch.

COLLAR Sew ends of collar together and pop over head.

Hints

Choosing Yarns

We recommend Rowan yarns, but as each dog takes only a small amount of yarn, any yarn can be used, either in different colours or thicknesses. If using thicker yarns, refer to the ball band for needle size but use needles that are at least two sizes smaller than recommended as the tension (gauge) needs to be tight so the stuffing doesn't show. If you use thicker yarn and larger needles, your dog will be considerably bigger. We feel that finer yarns create a more refined dog.

Knitting the Body and Head

When holding stitches to use later on in the pattern – for example, on the final row of the legs – work the last row on a spare double-pointed needle. This means you can pick up and knit or purl the stitches from either end of the needle.

After you have sewn up the back of the dog, there may be a hole at the nape of the neck (see page 173). Work a couple of Swiss darning stitches to fill this hole if need be.

Carefully follow the instructions when picking up and knitting the first row of the Neck and Head. The Right Side of Body is knitted first, then the Left Side of Body: the backbone of the dog is in the middle of this row. If the pieces are picked up incorrectly, the dog's head will be facing towards its tail.

Holes can develop around the short row shaping at the top of the head. When sewing on the ears, use the sewing-up end to patch up any holes. Swiss darning can also be used to cover up any untidy stitches.

Don't worry if your dog's neck is rather thickset; the collar is handy for giving the neck some shape. If need be, reduce the number of stitches on the collar.

Stuffing the Dog

Stuffing the dog is as important as the knitting. Depending on the breed, your dog will need either light, normal or dense stuffing. For instance, the Staffordshire Bull Terrier needs dense stuffing to look sturdy, while the Greyhound needs light stuffing to enhance its delicate shape. Refer to the photographs of each dog for guidance.

Use a knitting needle point to push the stuffing into the paws and into the nose of the dog. Even after the dog is sewn up you can manipulate the stuffing with a knitting needle. If the stitches are distorted you have overstuffed your dog.

We recommend using 100 per cent polyester or kapok stuffing, which is available from craft shops and online retailers. A dog takes 20–40g (¾–1½oz) of stuffing, depending on size.

Adding Personality

You can add real character to your own knitted dog. In each pattern we have said where to place the ears, but we suggest pinning on the ears to find the perfect position before sewing. For eyes, experiment with both the size and the placing of the French knots until you are happy with your dog's expression. For example, for a doleful expression add a tiny stitch in white at the corner of the eye. The nose is worked in satin stitch, normally about four stitches that get a little smaller towards the bottom of the nose.

An Important Note

The dogs aren't toys, so if you intend to give them to small children do not use pipecleaners in the construction. Instead, you will need to densely stuff the legs to make the dog stand up.

Methods

Abbreviations

alt alternate
approx approximately
beg begin(ning)
cm centimetre
cont continue
foll(s) follow(s)(ing)
g grams
icos including cast (bound) off stitch. After casting (binding) off the stated number of stitches, one stitch remains on the right-hand needle. This stitch is included in the number of the following group of stitches.
in inches
inc work into front and back of next stitch to increase by one stitch
k knit
k2(3)tog knit next two (three) stitches together
oz ounces
p purl
p2(3)tog purl next two (three) stitches together
rem remain(ing)
rep repeat
RS right side
sk2po slip one stitch, knit two stitches together, pass slipped stitch over
st(s) stitch(es)
st st stocking (stockinette) stitch
w&t wrap and turn. See Wrap and Turn Method, right.
WS wrong side
[ ] work instructions within square brackets as directed
* work instructions after asterisk(s) as directed

Colour Knitting

There are two main techniques for working with more than one colour in the same row of knitting – the intarsia technique and the Fair Isle technique. For some dogs, such as the Pointer and English Springer Spaniel, you use a combination of both methods, but here is a guide.

Intarsia Technique

This method is used when knitting individual, large blocks of colour. It is best to use a small ball (or long length) for each area of colour, otherwise the yarns will easily become tangled. When changing to a new colour, twist the yarns on the wrong side of the work to prevent holes forming.

When starting a new row, turn the knitting so that the yarns that are hanging from it untwist as much as possible. If you have several colours you may occasionally have to re-organize the yarns at the back of the knitting. Your work may look messy, but once the ends are all sewn in it will look fine.

Fair Isle (or Stranding) Technique

If there are no more than four stitches between colours you can use the Fair Isle technique. Begin knitting with the first colour, then drop this when you introduce the second colour. When you come to the first colour again, take it under the second colour to twist the yarns. When you come to the second colour again, take it over the first colour. The secret is not to pull the strands on the wrong side of the work too tightly or the work will pucker.

I-cord Technique

With double-pointed needles *knit a row. Slide the stitches to the other end of the needle. Do not turn the knitting. Repeat from *, pulling the yarn tight on the first stitch so that the knitting forms a tube.

Wrap and Turn Method (w&t)

Knit the number of stitches in the first short row. Slip the next stitch purlwise from the left-hand to the right-hand needle. Bring the yarn forward then slip the stitch back onto the left-hand needle. Return the yarn to the back. On a purl row use the same method, taking the yarn back then forward.

Loopy Stitch

On a knit row, knit one stitch as normal, but leave the stitch on the left-hand needle. Bring the yarn from the back to the front between the two needles. Loop the yarn around the fingers of your left hand; the number of fingers needed is specified in each pattern. Take the yarn back between the two needles to the back of the work. Knit the stitch from the left-hand needle as normal. You now have two stitches on the right-hand needle and a loop between them. Pass the first stitch over the second stitch to trap the loop, which is now secure. The end of the loop can be cut when finishing the dog.

When knitting the Bichon Frise, once the stitch is finished take the loop to the back of the work, so that the loop appears on the purl side.

As a guide, a 1-finger loop should be about 2cm (¾in) long, a 2-finger loop 3–4cm (1¼–1½in), a 3-finger loop 6cm (2½in), and a 4-finger loop 7cm (2¾in).

Sewing Up

Unless otherwise stated, sew up dogs on the RS using mattress stitch or on the WS using whip stitch: if sewn up on the WS then turn body RS out before stuffing. Note that legs are sewn up on the RS as they are too thin to turn RS out.

Most of the dogs are put together in a similar way, and instructions are given in all patterns. Generally, sew the head from nose to chin. Then one end of the tummy is attached at the chin and the other end either about 3cm (1¼in) below the tail, or where the back legs start. The seams are at the backs of the legs.

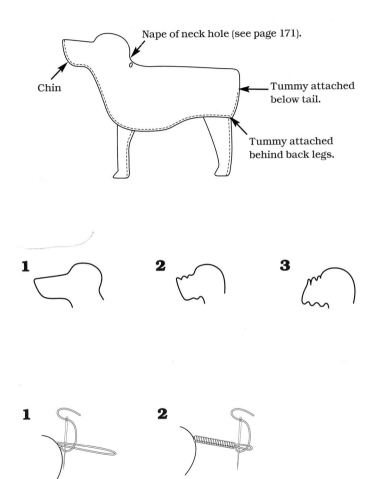

Nape of neck hole (see page 171).

Chin

Tummy attached below tail.

Tummy attached behind back legs.

Shar Pei Head

1 To shape the head, fold cast (bound) off row in half and sew from nose to chin. Stuff the head lightly.
2 Thread a tapestry needle with toffee yarn and fasten end to tip of nose, Take the yarn through the head to emerge at top back, and pull it up to form wrinkles.
3 Fold nose in on itself to form jowls and sew centre of jowls to end of muzzle.

Bedlington Tail

1 To make the tail, with smg make a 7cm (2¾in) loop where back meets bottom. Using the same yarn and starting at the end nearest the dog's bottom, work buttonhole stitch.
2 Cover the whole loop with tightly packed buttonhole stitches. When complete, thread the end of yarn up through the tail and trim.

Index of Dogs

80

86

92

98

104

Gun Dogs

112

118

124

130

Working

138

144

150

156

162

175

The Authors

Sally Muir and Joanna Osborne run their own knitwear business, Muir and Osborne. They export their knitwear to stores in the United States, Japan and Europe as well as selling to shops in the United Kingdom. Several pieces of their knitwear are in the permanent collection at the Victoria and Albert Museum, London.

Best in Show: 25 More Dogs to Knit is the follow-up to the bestselling *Best in Show: Knit Your Own Dog*.

Join our crafting community at LoveCrafts — we look forward to meeting you!

Acknowledgements

Thank you yet again to Rowan Yarns for both their generosity and fantastically dog-like selection of yarns. At the risk of sounding repetitive, we are delighted that we have had the same wonderful group of people working on this book, so, thank you again to Marilyn Wilson and Kate Haxell for their vigilance, Caroline Dawnay and Olivia Hunt for their resoluteness, Katie Cowan, Amy Christian, Laura Russell and everyone at Collins and Brown for their continuing support, and Holly Jolliffe for even better photographs. Thank you also to our families for putting up with it all.

Resources

All the dogs are knitted in Rowan yarns: for stockists please refer to the Rowan website www.knitrowan.com.

We recommend using 100 per cent polyester or kapok stuffing, available from craft shops and online retailers. A dog takes 20–40g (¾–1½oz) of stuffing, depending on size.

We are selling knitting kits for some of the dogs. The kits are packaged in a Best in Show knitting bag and contain yarn, all needles required, stuffing, pipecleaners, a silver-plated dog tag and a pattern.

For those who cannot knit but still want a dog, we are selling some of our dogs readymade. You can see the range of dogs on our website www.muirandosborne.co.uk.

Join our online
community at

www.knityourowndog.com

Best in Show

Knit your own dog then enter it into our online knitted dog show!